Congress and Arms Control

Other Titles in This Series

Westview Special Studies on International Relations and U.S. Foreign Policy

Congress and Arms Control
edited by Alan Platt and Lawrence Weiler

This volume focuses on the changing role of Congress with respect to various arms control issues—SALT, nonproliferation, arms sales, weapons procurement—and discusses such topical subjects as the role of secrecy in arms negotiations, the involvement of the Senate Foreign Relations Committee in the arms control policy process, European perspectives on congressional involvement in defense issues. The authors, practitioners as well as scholars, contribute significantly to the literature on both arms control and the Congress.

Alan Platt is special assistant for congressional relations, U.S. Arms Control and Disarmament Agency. He has previously been legislative assistant for foreign affairs to Senator Edmund Muskie and a research associate of Stanford University's Arms Control and Disarmament Program.

Lawrence Weiler has been counselor at the U.S. Arms Control and Disarmament Agency and professional coordinator of Stanford University's Arms Control and Disarmament Program.

Congress and Arms Control

edited by Alan Platt
and Lawrence D. Weiler

Westview Press / Boulder, Colorado

Westview Special Studies on
International Relations and U.S. Foreign Policy

Published in 1978 in the United States of America by
  Westview Press, Inc.
  5500 Central Avenue
  Boulder, Colorado 80301
  Frederick A. Praeger, Publisher

Library of Congress Cataloging in Publication Data
Main entry under title:
Congress and arms control.
  (Westview special studies on U.S. international relations and foreign policy)
  Includes index.
  1. Arms control—Addresses, essays, lectures. 2. United States—Military policy—
Addresses, essays, lectures. I. Platt, Alan. II. Weiler, Lawrence D.
HX1974.C683   327'.174'0973   77-28307
ISBN 0-89158-157-X

Printed and bound in the United States of America

Contents

Preface

Since the now historic ABM debate of 1969, the interest and involvement of Congress in foreign affairs in general and arms control in particular have grown significantly. Evidence of this abounds and is burgeoning daily. This current assertion of congressional power can be traced largely to two recent developments: the executive branch's loss of credibility in pursuing a highly unpopular war in Indochina, and the events surrounding President Nixon's 1974 resignation from office. The renaissance of a Congress unimpressed with executive branch preachments and proud of its own prerogatives can also be understood as a natural development in a country where the Constitution divides the power to regulate foreign affairs between the legislative and executive branches and where there has been a historical ebb and flow of congressional involvement in international affairs. However one explains it, since 1969 the legislative branch has played an increasingly influential role in making this country's foreign policy. During this period Congress has, *inter alia*, enacted unprecedented War Powers legislation, ended our involvement in Indochina, passed a revolutionary Budget Act, and terminated American assistance to Angola.

What has been the role of Congress in the arms control issues that have arisen since 1969? What problems and parameters are associated with congressional involvement in this policy area? This collection of essays is intended to shed light on the answers to these questions. The authors have not all addressed themselves to a single aspect of legislative involvement in arms control policy. Rather, each of the authors, a specialist in a particular field, has addressed a given subject from his own unique vantage point.

Common to all the essays, though, is the increasingly significant role of Congress in recent years in formulating arms control policy. This has not always been the case in the post-World War II period. Indeed, with a few notable exceptions such as the Limited Test Ban Treaty, the Non-Proliferation Treaty, and the ABM debate, Congress has not been actively involved in arms control policymaking, and the executive branch has dominated this very complex, highly classified, closely held aspect of our foreign policy. What is described and analyzed in each chapter of this volume is the increasing attention that Congress has been paying recently to various aspects of arms control policy. Whether it be SALT, arms sales, nuclear nonproliferation, or the defense budget, the legislative branch's involvement can no longer be ignored, avoided, or treated as an aberration. Now the role of Congress must be analyzed if one wants to understand how a given American policy decision on arms control has been reached.

For many, both in the United States and abroad, the growing role of Congress in arms control will require an adjustment in thinking. By providing concrete analyses of different aspects of congressional involvement in this field, this book, it is hoped, will facilitate the requisite rethinking. It is also hoped that this collection of essays will fill two notable gaps in the literature: one in studies of arms control, where the focus traditionally has been on the executive branch's arms control initiatives, and the other in the literature on Congress, where scant attention has been paid to legislative involvement in arms control policymaking.

* * *

This volume was prepared during the 1976-77 academic year, while I was a research associate of the Stanford Arms Control and Disarmament Program and Lawrence D. Weiler was its associate director. Initial versions of most of the papers in this collection were presented at monthly meetings of the Stanford Arms Control Faculty Seminar. I speak for all the contributors in saying that this collection would not have been possible without the initiative and continuing interest of John Wilson Lewis, director of the Stanford Arms Control and Disarmament Program. Special thanks are also due to the Ford Foundation for its generous support, to Muriel Bell and Mervyn Seldon for their help in editing this volume, and to Gerry Bowman and Barbara Johnson for assistance in preparing the manuscript.

Alan Platt
January 1978

The Contributors

Les Aspin is the congressman from the First District of Wisconsin. He serves on the Armed Services and Government Operations Committees.

Dick Clark is the senior senator from Iowa. He is a member of the Foreign Relations Committee and has served on its Arms Control Subcommittee.

Alan Cranston is the senior senator from California. He is the Democratic Whip and chairman of the Veterans Affairs Committee.

Thomas Dine is currently the director of the National Security Task Force of the Senate Budget Committee. He has previously been legislative assistant for foreign affairs to Senator Frank Church and research associate of the Program on Science and International Affairs, Harvard University.

Warren Donnelly has worked for many years as senior specialist in the Environment and Natural Resources Policy Division of the Congressional Research Service, Library of Congress.

Philip Farley was deputy director of the Arms Control and Disarmament Agency and served as alternate U.S. representative for Strategic Arms Limitation Talks with the Soviet Union from 1969 to 1973. After a period as a senior fellow with the Brookings Institution and then as visiting scholar with

Stanford University's Arms Control and Disarmament Program, Farley has returned to government service as deputy special representative for nonproliferation negotiations, Department of State.

Alton Frye is currently a senior fellow of the Council on Foreign Relations and director of the Institute for Congress Project, Carnegie Endowment for International Peace. He has previously been administrative assistant to Senator Edward Brooke and a staff member of the Rand Corporation.

Kurt J. Lauk holds a Ph.D. from the University of Kiel (West Germany) and an M.A. in Business Administration from Stanford University. He has served as a consultant on defense affairs to West Germany's Christian Democratic Party and currently works in Germany as a representative of the Boston Consulting Group.

John Wilson Lewis is the William Haas Professor of Chinese Politics and director of the Arms Control and Disarmament Program at Stanford University. He also serves as a consultant to the Senate Select Committee on Intelligence.

Alan Platt is special assistant for congressional relations, U.S. Arms Control and Disarmament Agency. He has previously been legislative assistant for foreign affairs to Senator Edmund Muskie and research associate of Stanford University's Arms Control and Disarmament Program.

Lawrence Weiler was formerly adjunct professor of political science and associate director of the Arms Control and Disarmament Program, Stanford University. Before that he was counselor of the Arms Control and Disarmament Agency.

Abbreviations

ABM	Antiballistic Missile
ACDA	Arms Control and Disarmament Agency
AEC	Atomic Energy Commission
AID	Agency for International Development
ALCM	Air-Launched Cruise Missile
AWACS	Airborne Warning and Control System
FBS	Forward-Based Systems
FMS	Foreign Military Sales
IAEA	International Atomic Energy Agency
ICBM	Intercontinental Ballistic Missile
IRBM	Intermediate-Range Ballistic Missile
MAP	Military Assistance Program
MBFR	Mutual Balanced Force Reductions (for Central Europe)
MIRV	Multiple Independently Targetable Reentry Vehicle
MLBM	Modern Large Ballistic Missile
MRBM	Medium-Range Ballistic Missile
NATO	North Atlantic Treaty Organization
NEPA	National Environmental Protection Act
NPT	Non-Proliferation Treaty
OTA	Office of Technology Assessment
PNE	Peaceful Nuclear Explosions
RCA	Riot-Control Agents
SALT	Strategic Arms Limitation Talks
SLBM	Submarine-Launched Ballistic Missile

1
Congress and Arms Control: A Historical Perspective, 1969-1976

Alan Platt

On August 6, 1969, after the most searching congressional examination of any weapons program since World War II, the United States Senate approved the deployment of an Antiballistic Missile System (ABM) by a one-vote margin.[1] Before the vote numerous executive branch officials and outside experts were questioned intensively by several committees about the advantages and drawbacks of the proposed new system. Alternative policies were offered and debated, sometimes heatedly. The administration's ABM proposal, though ultimately approved, was subjected to such exhaustive scrutiny during the five weeks of debate that many senators proclaimed the arrival of a new era: Congress had become an active participant in the making of national security policy. Nor were the senators alone; Murray Marder, veteran diplomatic correspondent of the *Washington Post,* wrote dramatically about the first session of the 91st Congress:

The views in this chapter are solely those of the author. The Arms Control and Disarmament Agency, where the author is special assistant for congressional relations, bears no responsibility for the contents of this article.

1

Groundwork for a non-violent rebellion inside the American Establishment was begun during the session of Congress that ended Tuesday. Young militants would hoot at the sedate inhouse struggle. But historians do not. They will watch with scholarly fascination to see if the decade of the 70's produces only a sham revolt or a reapportionment of power between the executive and the legislative branches on matters of war and peace. The challengers of unquestioned executive branch primacy went on to question intended actions they never dreamed of seriously disputing in years past. They contested and lost by only one vote, the decision to develop an antiballistic missile system.[2]

Tom Halsted, then chief anti-ABM lobbyist for the Council for a Livable World, summarized the new situation more succinctly: "The ABM debates have brought about some permanent changes. The public has become involved to an important degree in national security decisionmaking. The days of Congressional rubber-stamping may be over."[3]

Underlying these remarks was the feeling, held widely both inside and outside Congress, that from the dawn of the nuclear age in 1945 until the ABM debate, the legislative branch had largely relinquished oversight responsibility on national security issues to the executive, particularly in arms control matters.[4] Between 1945 and 1969 few members of Congress had been actively involved in the formulation of arms control policy; Congress had generally been content with *pro forma* evaluation of the executive's annual defense requests, save for an occasional increase in appropriations for a particular weapons system and a still more occasional marginal cut in the Pentagon's annual budget in the name of fiscal prudence. To be sure, there were some exceptions to this pattern of congressional rubber-stamping. But Congress's role in the passage of the McMahon Act of 1954, its interest in the 1956-58 manned bomber versus missile controversy, and its active support of the 1963 Limited Test Ban and the 1968 Non-Proliferation Treaty stand out precisely as exceptions that prove the rule.

The 1969 ABM debate led many members of Congress to believe that henceforth they would play a consistently more active role in formulating arms control policies. No longer, many felt, would executive spokesmen be able to testify behind closed doors before docilely supportive committees. No longer would members of Congress and their staffs lack the knowledge to discuss strategic doctrine and weapons policies. No longer would the excutive be the sole source of technical information on complex military matters. And most important, no longer could the executive assume that its defense policies and budget requests would receive unquestioning support. John Sherman Cooper, a senior member of the Senate Foreign Relations Committee, expressed the feeling of many of his colleagues when he philosophically reflected in a speech on the Senate floor: "The responsibility for national security rests with the Congress as well as with the executive branch of government. We respect the President's grave responsibilities, but the Constitution calls for a joint judgment. It is a trust given the Congress by the people."[5]

Since the ABM debate, how has Congress fulfilled this trust? Was the ABM debate indeed a watershed, or an aberrant effort without lasting consequence? To the extent that Congress has been involved in arms control policy during the last several years, what has its influence been? Why has Congress been more involved in some arms control issues than others? What are the prospects for future congressional participation in arms control policymaking?

Because of the jurisdictional lines drawn by the congressional committee structure, there are from a legislative point of view two principal components of arms control policy: (1) weapons policy, which includes research, development, testing, evaluation, procurement, deployment, and cost; and (2) foreign policy, which includes arms negotiations with other nations.[6] The first falls within the purview of the Senate and House Armed Services, Appropriations, and Budget Committees,[7] while the second is considered primarily by the Senate Foreign Relations Committee and the House International Relations Committee (known until January 1975 as the House Foreign Affairs Committee), but also by the Armed Services Committees of the two houses.

Congress and Weapons Policies

Concerning weapons policies, analysts differ considerably

in their assessment of the role of Congress since 1969. Some, like Edward Laurance, believe that congressional involvement in formulating U.S. weapons policies during these years represents "a step-level change" from the past.[8] Contrasting congressional treatment of the defense budget during 1945-67 with 1968-74, Laurance demonstrates in quantitative terms how congressional involvement has changed. Specifically, since 1967 he finds measurable increases in:

1. the amount of time members of Congress spent at hearings and working on legislation concerned with weapons policies;
2. the number of witnesses from outside the executive branch called to testify before Congress on weapons policies and the number of witnesses presenting views different from those of the executive branch;
3. the number and educational level of congressional staff members dealing with weapons policies;
4. congressional use of outside consultants knowledgeable about arms control, many of them former executive branch employees capable of providing independent technical analysis;
5. the amount of information relating to arms control issues disseminated by Congress as a result of vastly expanded committee reports;
6. the number of amendments to reduce spending offered to the annual Military Procurement Authorization and Appropriations bills;
7. the number of committees scrutinizing weapons policies.

It should be added that since 1969 Congress has attempted to upgrade the capacity of two existing organizations—the General Accounting Office and the Congressional Research Service of the Library of Congress—to investigate weapons programs. Congress also created two new organizations to provide in-depth analyses of various weapons systems—the Office of Technology Assessment and the Congressional Budget Office.[9]

Following the ABM debate, there was also a concerted movement outside government to heighten congressional knowledge of United States weapons policies and congressional involvement in them. Several private organizations—the Arms Control Association, Federation of American Scientists, Members of Congress for Peace through Law, Council for a Livable World, and the Center for Defense Information—were either organized or activated to supply members of Congress with detailed information about arms control and defense policies.

For Laurance and others these developments taken together have led to a "new defense policy system," with Congress scrutinizing and modifying executive weapons policies to an unprecedented extent.[10] Edward Laurance, Lawrence Korb, et al. have not only described the characteristics of the "new system," but have also enumerated some of the system's arms control "outputs" such as a slowdown in procurement of the B-1 bomber and the patrol frigate and significant reductions in United States troop levels abroad. In addition, they have shown that from 1969 to 1976 Congress has reduced the executive's annual defense request by more than $5 billion on the average and, as Laurance points out, these figures ignore "the feedback loop which continually causes the Department of Defense to change [its weapons requests] in anticipation of Congressional action."[11]

Other analysts of the defense policymaking process, such as Les Aspin and Robert Benson, agree that weapons proposals have been subjected to intensifying congressional scrutiny in recent years and concede that such scrutiny is likely to increase owing to the establishment of Senate and House Budget Committees.[12] These analysts argue, however, that increased congressional involvement has not led to diminished expenditures on arms. Indeed, Aspin, Benson, et al. point out that congressional appropriations for defense have grown from $69 billion in Fiscal Year 1970 to $116.6 billion for Fiscal 1978, the latter figure approved in September 1977 under the Congress's new budgetary procedures.[13] In addition, Aspin, Benson, et al. note that, with the possible exception of ABM, which was negotiated away with the Soviets in significant part due to legislative pressure, Congress has not rejected a single major weapons system proposed by the executive since 1969.

Benson, who thinks the government should spend more money on cities and less on defense, summarizes the situation as follows: Congress "is doing an improved job of scrutinizing military programs but has remained impotent in cancelling new programs its members will consider ill advised. Overall, Congress has very little impact on military expenditure levels. Presidents regularly succeed in getting approved virtually the full range of military programs they request from Congress."[14]

In short, there is considerable disagreement about the impact on defense expenditures of increased congressional involvement in weapons policy. What is not in dispute, though, is Congress's intensified scrutiny of weapons policies since the ABM debate of 1969.

Congress and Arms Control Negotiations

With regard to the other principal component of United States arms control policy—arms negotiations with foreign countries—the pattern has not changed significantly since World War II. The executive formulates, negotiates, and presents national policy, and Congress votes yes. During the last eight years three major arms control treaties have been concluded with the Soviets: the 1972 ABM Treaty, the 1974 Threshold Nuclear Test Limitation Treaty, and the 1976 Treaty to Limit Peaceful Nuclear Explosions.[15] In addition, in 1972 following the first round of Strategic Arms Limitation Talks, known as SALT I, an Interim Agreement to Limit Offensive Arms was concluded with the Soviets; in 1974 a Protocol to the ABM Treaty was agreed to; and since 1973 talks with the Soviets aiming at a second SALT accord and an agreement to limit NATO and Warsaw Pact forces in Central Europe have continued. Furthermore, both bilateral and multilateral discussions have been held on preventing the spread of nuclear weapons and banning all nuclear testing.

In each of these cases the pattern of executive-legislative relations has been the same: the executive has formulated the national negotiating posture; informed and consulted with Congress very selectively, most closely after a treaty has been concluded; and, while the negotiations were in progress, expected and received legislative support. The Congress, for its part, made little effort in subcommittee, full committee, or in either house as a whole to analyze, debate, or explore alternative policies. Congress was most actively involved in these arms negotiations after it was called on to ratify an already concluded treaty. Typically, most members of the Senate and House opted not even to inform themselves about the precise issues under discussion during the negotiations themselves. In short, with respect to formulating policy for arms negotiations since 1969, Congress's performance has generally been a far cry from the "joint judgment" urged by Senator Cooper.

SALT I is a case in point. The week before the first round of the talks began, on November 12, 1969, Senator Albert Gore, chairman of the Foreign Relations Subcommittee on Arms Control, announced the cancellation of a scheduled closed-door subcommittee briefing on SALT. Gerard Smith, director of the Arms Control and Disarmament Agency (ACDA), had telephoned Gore to say that he was not free to discuss SALT policy with members of Congress. Nettled by the conversation, Gore affirmed Congress's responsibility in foreign affairs and expressed the fervent hope that thereafter Congress would play an active role in SALT. Gore suggested also that it would be in the Nixon administration's interest to encourage more active congressional involvement in foreign affairs. After Gore's statement, it was reported that before cancelling the briefing, Smith had talked to the presidential assistant for national security affairs, Henry Kissinger, and that the White House had vetoed Smith's appearance before the subcommittee.[16]

The following day, after a breakfast meeting with President Nixon, Senate Majority Leader Mike Mansfield announced that there had been a "misunderstanding," which he thought was now "cleared up." But on the same day President Nixon, while acknowledging the importance of keeping the Senate fully informed on SALT, publicly declared it "vital that we recognize that the position of our negotiators not be weakened or compromised by discussions that might take place here [in Congress]."[17]

The unavailability of a key executive branch official to brief Congress on SALT; the subsequent ineffectual grumbling of members of the Senate Foreign Relations Committee (e. g., Gore, Cooper, Case) about the cancelled Smith hearing and about Congress's inadequate information on national security matters; the seeming indifference in the House of Representatives to SALT I; the unconvincing lip service paid by the Nixon administration to the idea of keeping Congress informed about SALT—this series of events, which took place before the first SALT session had even been convened, was in many ways characteristic of executive-legislative relations throughout SALT I, from November 1969 to May 1972. The executive verbally conceded that Congress should be fully informed and closely involved in SALT, while "briefing" Congress in only a sporadic and *pro forma* way, with the key official, Kissinger, unavailable to testify before Congress. The legislative branch, in turn, periodically complained about inadequate information, consultation, and involvement regarding SALT, but did little to force a change. Save for occasional individual private efforts by a few senators, notably Cooper and Henry Jackson, to keep themselves informed, Congress remained generally unaware of the details of American SALT policy and the progress of the negotiations. In short, as John Newhouse, the principal chronicler of SALT I, has written: "Most important SALT decisions [were] taken without reference to Congress."[18]

With the initialing of the accords in Moscow in May 1972, the picture changed. The agreement to limit ABMs was embodied in a formal treaty, thus requiring ratification by two-thirds of the Senate. And, whereas the Interim Agreement to Limit Offensive Weapons was an executive agreement rather than a treaty, approval by both houses of Congress was required by the 1961 legislation that created ACDA.[19] Thus the Nixon administration was obliged to work closely with Congress once the SALT I accords were signed; and Congress, for its part, could not escape ratification of the SALT I agreements.

To dramatize the importance of the accords, half an hour after returning to Washington from Moscow on June 1, President Nixon addressed a specially convened joint session of Congress. He described the substance of the SALT agreements and made it clear that administration officials were willing to spend as much time as necessary to inform members of the Senate and House about them.

On June 15, accordingly, the president and Kissinger spent more than two hours in the White House, briefing some 120 senators and representatives on the details of the accords. At one point Nixon noted that executive privilege precluded Kissinger's testifying before Congress on behalf of the agreements. However, Nixon added,

> since this is really an unprecedented situation, it seemed to me that it was important that he appear before the members of Congress in this format. This in on the record. What we are asking for here . . . is cooperation and not just rubber-stamping by the House and the Senate. That is essential because there must be follow-through on this, and the members of the House and Senate, it seems to me, must be convinced that they played a role . . . and will continue to play a role in this very, very important field of arms control.[20]

Kissinger thereupon spelled out the rationale and terms of the SALT I accords. During the question-and-answer period Senator Claiborne Pell, a senior member of the Senate Foreign Relations Committee, revealingly inquired, "Why, in this set of negotiations, was the constitutionally normal course of Congressional consultation, advice as well as consent, not engaged in?" Kissinger lamely replied: "As for the process of consultation, this is not my specialty, but it has been my understanding that Mr. [Gerard] Smith and the appropriate secretaries have been in close consultation."[21]

Congressional scrutiny of the SALT I accords was dominated by Senator Jackson. The accords were first referred to Foreign Relations, the congressional committee with direct responsibility for approving treaties. But that committee's hearings were anything but searching.[22] The approach was very different in the Armed Services Committee, which decided to hold hearings on the accords' military implications. Several members of Armed Services, led by Senator Jackson, seized the occasion to explore in depth not only the accords under consideration but also the entire SALT policymaking process and overall strategic balance between the United States and the Soviet Union. To Jackson the administration seemed to have been overanxious to achieve an arms control agreement. Specifically, he feared that the Interim Agreement froze the United States in a position of serious numerical inferiority in both Intercontinental Ballistic Missiles (ICBMs) and Submarine-Launched Ballistic Missiles (SLBMs), while leaving the Soviets free to achieve parity with the United States in Multiple Independently Targetable Reentry Vehicles (MIRVs). He believed there was a real risk that ratifying the Interim Agreement would permit the Soviet Union to develop a first-strike capability during the agreement's five-year duration.

During the Armed Services Committee hearings in June 1972, Senator Jackson also criticized the way the administration had dealt with Congress on SALT I. He berated executive witnesses for not being "forthcoming" with Congress on strategic arms issues; for selectively declassifying information supportive of its positions; for hiding relevant negotiating details and texts from Congress; and, in general, for not leveling with Congress until the talks were completed.[23]

To prevent a repetition of these putative mistakes in subsequent SALT negotiations, Jackson proposed an amendment, "policy guidance from the Congress," to the legislation ratifying the Interim Agreement. Among other things the Jackson Amendment called for numerical equality in future strategic arms agreements. Equality referred both to ICBMs and SLBMs, which were covered in the accord and in which the United States held a substantial lead. The amendment also called for "the maintenance of a vigorous research and development program" in support of a "prudent strategic posture."[24] In the weeks following Jackson's introduction of his amendment, several senators (e. g., J. William Fulbright, Edmund Muskie, Stuart Symington) futilely attempted to change its thrust. Other like-minded senators (e. g., Edward Brooke, Harold Hughes, Mike Mansfield) tried with little success to undercut the amendment by adding language of their own to the pending legislation.

Finally, after several weeks of extensive and at times acrimonious debate, the Senate ratified the Interim Agreement by a vote of 88-2, after adopting the Jackson Amendment by

a vote of 56-35. As finally enacted, the amendment requested the
president in future SALT negotiations to seek a treaty that
would not limit the United States "to levels of intercontinental
strategic forces inferior to the limits provided for the Soviet
Union." The House had already passed ratifying legislation—
after a one-hour *pro forma* debate—by a vote of 329-7.
Accordingly, on September 30 the president signed into law the
legislation, as amended by Senator Jackson, that ratified the
Interim Agreement.

In summary, legislative involvement in SALT I policymaking changed markedly once the ABM Treaty and the
Interim Agreement were initialed in Moscow and submitted to
Congress for approval. Until then, the executive monopolized
the formulation of SALT policy, while members of Congress,
sporadically briefed in a *pro forma* way, passively supported
the executive. Following the Moscow summit, the executive
made a sustained effort to consult closely with Congress. A few
members of Congress seized this opportunity to question in
depth the executive officials closest to the SALT negotiations,
notably Henry Kissinger, and to scrutinize and modify United
States SALT policy.

The Congressional Role after SALT I, 1972-1976

Following ratification of the SALT I accords in September
1972, both the executive and the legislative branches reverted to
form. Specifically, on November 21, 1972, the first SALT II
session convened in Geneva, and in the 1972-76 period, policy
for the SALT talks was made basically by the executive branch,
with minimal consultation of Congress, which by and large
was content to acquiesce in adminstration initiatives. This is
not to deny the interest and even influence, albeit limited, of
such senators as Jackson, Case, Muskie, Alan Cranston, Hubert
Humphrey, Charles Mathias, and John Stennis on SALT II.
Nor is it to ignore the introduction of several sense-of-the-
Senate resolutions concerning strategic arms limitations (none
passed) or the enactment in 1975 of legislation requiring an
executive written report on the potential impact of strategic
weapons programs on arms control.[25] Overall, however,

between 1972 and 1976, Congress was not an active participant in SALT II policymaking. Most members of Congress did not keep in touch with the details of the issues under negotiation, let alone challenge the underlying bases for various American stances or affect policy directly by legislation. In short, the executive dominated SALT II in these years much as it did SALT I.

Why was Congress more actively involved in trying to analyze programs from 1969 to 1976 than in scrutinizing arms control negotiations? The answer lies in the operational patterns and attitudes of the executive and legislative branches toward these dual aspects of arms control policy.

It is no secret that the foreign, and to some extent defense, policies of both the Nixon and Ford administrations were shaped largely by one man, Henry Kissinger. Early in 1969, with President Nixon's concurrence, Kissinger established a complex, closed system to formulate policy for arms negotiations with other countries. The decision-making machinery Kissinger set up allowed him to shape the issues under consideration; to enumerate the various alternatives; and ultimately to present choices to the president for his decision. The most unusual characteristic of this policymaking process was not that the ultimate decisions were made privately by the president, but that the shape of the issues under discussion was kept secret from much of the government, including most of the executive branch and usually all of Congress. To put it another way, during the Kissinger period those normally responsible for shaping and debating an issue—in both the executive and legislative branches—were generally unable to identify alternative considerations or the grounds on which choices were made.[26]

Created in part to avoid leaks, in part to maximize Kissinger's influence on the president, this closed system of policymaking effectively precluded members of Congress from active involvement in formulating American negotiating policies. The Kissinger system was characterized by:

1. *pro forma* consultation with the responsible Congressional committees (e.g., Senate Foreign Relations,

House International Relations, Senate and House
Armed Services);
2. refusal to give Congress the texts of the basic United
   States proposals;
3. a disinclination to keep Congress informed about
   changes in American positions during negotiations;
4. discouragement of congressional debate on key policy
   issues involved in the negotiations, including Soviet
   counterproposals.[27]

To be sure, had a large number of senators and representatives, either individually or collectively, challenged their exclusion from this process, the closed system might have been breached. But most members of Congress opted not to do so.[28] Some felt that formulating policy for arms talks with other nations was a responsibility residing exclusively with the executive branch and with the president as commander-in-chief. Efforts to involve Congress, they felt, could only hamper, not help. Others believed it impractical for Congress to oversee day-to-day developments in negotiations and felt they would have ample opportunity to formulate and present their views once an agreement was submitted to Congress for ratification. Still others felt that neither they nor the available staff support had the background and expertise to contribute usefully in this area. Perhaps most important, virtually no member of Congress felt compelling constituent pressure to play a more active role in formulating arms negotiations policy. Indeed, most senators and representatives were under pressure from their constituents to focus their energies on such urgent matters as the domestic economy and Vietnam, fully expecting that by remaining uninvolved they would share the credit if the negotiations proved successful and avoid blame if they foundered.[29]

Reinforcing these predilections was a lack of leadership on arms control by the two committees directly charged with overseeing United States foreign policy—Foreign Relations in the Senate, International Relations in the House. The Senate committee, chaired by J. William Fulbright from 1969 to 1974 and John Sparkman thereafter, was disinclined to participate actively in formulating arms control policy. Both Fulbright and Sparkman preferred to let the president and the executive bureaucracy, headed by Kissinger, dominate this area of our foreign relations.

The Senate Foreign Relations Committee's passive-supportive attitude was paralleled in the House International Relations Committee. Following the lead of its chairman, Thomas "Doc" Morgan, the House committee gave the executive consistent, unquestioning support for its arms negotiations policies. However, it should be noted that during the last three years of his tenure, 1973-76, Chairman Morgan permitted the various subcommittee chairmen an increasing degree of autonomy. Congressman Clement Zablocki, chairman of the Subcommittee on National Security Policy and Scientific Developments, used this latitude to look closely at several aspects of arms control policy. In 1974 he published an in-depth study of the Arms Control and Disarmament Agency and its relation to Congress.[30]

Many of the constitutional and political considerations just enumerated with regard to arms negotiations have not pertained to weapons policy. That legislative participation in this area is legitimate and appropriate has not been questioned. Congress's authority is clearly spelled out in Article I of the Constitution, which states that "no money shall be drawn from the Treasury but on Consequence of Appropriations made by Law; and a regular Statement and Account of Receipts and Expenditures of all public Money shall be published from time to time." In other words, taxpayers' money cannot be spent without a congressional appropriation, and these appropriations must be made public. It is clear that the framers of the Constitution intended this power of the purse to be used extensively with regard to defense. Besides the appropriations clause, Article I provides that Congress shall "provide for the common defense," and Articles 12, 13, and 14 give Congress the power "to raise and support armies," "to provide and maintain a navy," and "to make rules for the government and regulation of land and naval forces."

With the Constitution as justification, Congress in recent years has increased the number of items in the annual defense budget that have to pass through each house in two stages: first, authorization by the Senate and House Armed Services Committees; second, appropriation by the relevant subcommittees of the Appropriations Committees. In addition, all appropriations for weapons systems must now come under the annual ceiling set on all defense expenditures by the Budget Committees. Put another way, so far as weapons programs are concerned, the executive has not been able to create the kind of closed system that operated for arms control negotiations. Each year executive officials have had to appear before the relevant congressional committees and defend in both open and closed sessions their proposed weapons programs. There has been no way to avoid this.

This is not to say that Congress will necessarily scrutinize weapons programs closely, let alone challenge the executive branch's proposals. Indeed, as was evident between 1945 and 1969, the authorization and appropriations processes do not ensure active congressional participation in weapons policy-making. Congressional reviews can be mere rituals that rubber-stamp executive policies. That in recent years Congress has been increasingly assertive regarding weapons policies can be directly attributed to several factors: the 1969 ABM experience; disillusionment with previous weapons programs, particularly those involving huge cost overruns; rising concern for reordering national priorities; an increasingly active and skeptical Senate Armed Services Research and Development Subcommittee; and the new budgetary procedures. All these factors have had a cumulative effect. Since 1969 congressional participation in weapons policymaking has grown, and the trend seems likely to continue.

In the future, congressional participation in arms negotiation policies also is likely to grow. Indeed, such a trend was already apparent in 1977 as the Foreign Relations and Armed Services Committees of both houses perceptibly intensified their oversight of U.S. SALT II policy. And as staff resources on arms control issues increase both inside and outside the legislative branch; as members of Congress, as a result, become more informed and comfortable with the complexities and trade-offs associated with these issues; as constituents step up the pressure on their elected representatives to spend tax dollars more prudently, including those spent on defense—increased congressional participation in the various aspects of the arms control policymaking process seems inevitable. This development is by no means unhealthy or undesirable, for an activist Congress can and should play a central role in formulating this country's arms control policies.

Notes

1. Some of the following material appears in the author's forthcoming work, *The U.S. Senate and Strategic Arms Policy, 1969-1977* (Boulder, Colo., 1978).

2. *Washington Post*, December 27, 1969, p. A-2.

3. Thomas Halsted, "Lobbying Against the ABM, 1967-70," *Bulletin of the Atomic Scientists* 27 (April 1971): 28.

4. For the purposes of this paper, the term arms control "involves limitations on the numbers or types of armaments or armed forces, on their deployment or disposition, or on the use of particular types of armaments." This definition is borrowed from the Stanford University Arms Control Group's *International Arms Control: Issues and Agreements,* John H. Barton and Lawrence D. Weiler, eds. (Stanford, Calif., 1976), p. 3, n. 1.

5. *Congressional Record,* August 6, 1969, S-22488.

6. See Anne Cahn, "The Role of Congress and the Public in Arms Control" (Paper, Harvard University, September 1974), p. 2.

7. Under the Budget Reform Act of 1974 the Senate and House Budget Committees were established in 1975.

8. Edward Laurance, "The Changing Role of Congress in Defense Policy-Making," *Journal of Conflict Resolution* 20 (June 1976): 213-53.

9. For additional indicators of increased congressional involvement in arms control policy in recent years, see Anne Cahn, *Congress, Military Affairs and Information*, Sage Publication no. 04-017 (Beverly Hills, Calif., 1974), pp. 46-48.

10. See, for example, Lawrence Korb, "The Bicentennial Defense Budget: A Critical Appraisal," *Armed Forces and Society* 2 (November 1975):128-39.

11. Laurance, "Changing Role of Congress," p. 250.

12. Les Aspin, "The Defense Budget and Foreign Policy: The Role of Congress," *Daedalus* 104 (Summer 1975): 155-74, and Roberts Benson, "The Military on Capitol Hill: Prospects in the Quest for Funds," *Annals of the American Academy of Political and Social*

Science, March 1973, pp. 48-58.

13. For a detailed discussion of Congress's treatment of recent defense budgets, see Richard Cronin, *An Analysis of Congressional Reductions in the Defense Budget: Fiscal Years 1971-76.* Library of Congress Publication no. 76-205F (Washington, D.C., 1976).

14. Benson, "Military on Capitol Hill," p. 48.

15. Besides these agreements, a Treaty Banning Emplacement of Weapons of Mass Destruction on the Seabed was concluded in 1971; an Agreement to Reduce the Risk of Outbreak of Nuclear War was concluded in 1971; the Hot-Line Agreement was updated in 1971; a Biological Warfare Convention was negotiated in 1972; and an Agreement on the Prevention of Nuclear War was concluded in 1973.

16. *Washington Post*, November 13, 1969.

17. *New York Times*, November 14, 1969.

18. John Newhouse, *Cold Dawn: The Story of SALT* (New York, 1973), p. 32. For further discussion of executive dominance of SALT I, see Lawrence Weiler, *The Arms Race, Secret Negotiations and the Congress*, Occasional Paper no. 12, The Stanley Foundation (Muscatine, Ia., 1976).

19. The statute creating ACDA provides that "no action shall be taken under this or any law that will obligate the United States to disarm or to reduce or to limit the Armed Forces or armaments of the United States, except pursuant to the treaty-making power of the President under the Constitution unless authorized by further affirmative legislation by the Congress of the United States." *U.S. Statutes at Large*, vol. 75, 87th Cong., 1st sess., p. 631.

20. "Remarks of the President at a Congressional Briefing on the Arms Limitation Treaty and Agreement, June 15, 1972." White House Press Release, June 15, 1972.

21. "The White House, Question and Answer Session After a Briefing by Dr. Henry Kissinger, Assistant to the President for National Security Affairs, June 15, 1972." White House Press Release, June 15, 1972.

22. See U.S., Congress, Senate, Committee on Foreign Relations, *Hearings on the Strategic Arms Limitation Agreements*, 92nd Cong., 2nd sess., June-July 1972.

23. U.S., Congress, Senate, Committee on Armed Services, *Hearings on the Military Implications of the Treaty on the Limitations of Anti-Ballistic Missile Systems and the Interim Agreement on Limitation of Strategic Offensive Arms*, 92nd Cong., 2nd sess., June-July 1972, pp. 296-305, 310-311, 407-8.

24. The full text of the Jackson Amendment is reprinted in *Strategic Arms Limitation Talks (SALT): Legislative History of the*

Jackson Amendment (Washington, D.C., 1972), pp. 1-11.

25. In 1975-76 the executive branch complied with the letter but not the spirit of the 1975 law mandating arms control impact statements. The reports to Congress were so brief and noncommittal that, as Congressman Les Aspin put it, they were "a farce." *New York Times,* September 12, 1976.

26. For a detailed discussion of Kissinger's closed decision-making system regarding SALT, see Graham Allison, *An Overview of the Commission on the Organization of the Government for the Conduct of Foreign Policy* (Washington, D.C., 1975), pp. 76-79.

27. See Weiler, *The Arms Race,* pp. 13-15.

28. Two notable exceptions were Senators Cooper and Jackson. Early in SALT I, Cooper, dissatisfied with the lack of congressional involvement, tried to persuade the administration to allow senators to participate directly in the negotiations—either as observers or as official members of the American delegation. He was rebuffed. Despite the sympathetic response of several executive officials, including chief SALT negotiator Gerard Smith, Kissinger strongly opposed any congressional participation in the negotiations, and in this area Kissinger dictated administration policy, as was strikingly shown. Just before the May 1972 summit, Senate Majority Leader Mansfield proposed to President Nixon that he (Mansfield) and Senators Cooper, Jackson, and Stennis accompany the president to Moscow for the signing of the SALT I accords. Nixon was initially enthusiastic about the idea, but after conferring with Kissinger, he turned Mansfield down.

29. For a revealing discussion of prevalent congressional thinking about the preeminent role of the president in arms negotiations in particular and national security affairs in general, see the 1970 Senate discussion of the MIRV issue. *Congressional Record,* April 9, 1970, S-11045-57.

30. See U.S., Congress, House, Committee on Foreign Affairs, *Review of Arms Control Legislation and Organization, a Report Prepared for the Subcommittee on National Security Policy and Scientific Developments, September 1974,* 93rd Cong., 2d sess., 1974.

2
The Congressional Resource Problem

Alton Frye

Like love, arms control is a many-splendored thing. Intellectuals, enamored of complexity, are fond of arms control. Politicians, driven by reality, also find themselves frequently embracing the subject. In the Congress of the United States, that mixing bowl of interests and affections, arms control has long been the object of a love-hate relationship. It is a many-faceted relationship and to analyze it thoroughly, one must examine the congressional role in arms control policy making from a variety of perspectives.

In attempting such an analysis, we would do well to avoid rigid conceptions of the legislative and executive roles in American foreign policy. James Madison and other Federalists recorded many truths regarding those roles, and it is important to relearn their Constitutional counsel. But is is also crucial to apply that counsel intelligently to modern circumstances, in which the requirements of national security and of collaboration between legislature and executive have both changed significantly.

Surprisingly for an issue of such executive flavor and technical intricacy, arms control is a field in which Congress has been extremely active for many years. Indeed, largely though the work of Senator Hubert Humphrey and the Senate Foreign Relations Subcommittee on Disarmament, it was Congress which in 1961 created arms control as a separate category of executive responsibility. In the years since the creation of the Arms Control and Disarmament Agency (ACDA), Congress has remained an active arena in which the major questions of controlling both nuclear and conventional arms have figured prominently.

We may delineate Congress's role in this realm in terms of several basic functions. These functions intersect and overlap, but they are sufficiently distinct to warrant enumeration: (1) assessing executive plans, programs, and proposals related to arms control; (2) flushing out arms control issues that have been neglected or buried in the bureaucracy; (3) ensuring that the full range of responsible views is heard on major arms control questions; (4) amplifying citizen and legislative concerns about particular arms control problems; and (5) signaling to both the executive branch and foreign observers the likely political latitude and congressional support available to arms control negotiators. These and other relevant functions are sometimes performed only sporadically or even inadvertently, but they characterize a number of the fundamental effects of congressional involvement in arms control matters.

In evaluating how and how well Congress performs such functions, it is helpful to keep in mind the observation of Congressman Les Aspin that Congress is "neither a RAND Corporation nor a Brookings Institution." Legislative participation in complex policy problems is not inherently analytic but political, although the contrast between these approaches may not be so great as is sometimes assumed.[1] Analysis and politics share a concern for the consequences of particular policies for a community's constituent elements, but politicians are understandably prone to dwell upon the implications for their individual constituencies rather than the effects on the nation as a whole. The nature of arms control issues, however, encourages a national rather than a local focus even among legislators. Although the potential impact of various arms control agreements varies from region to region, with respect to possible economic dislocations caused by cutbacks in weapons, arms control issues generally have elicited a "national interest perspective" from the congressmen and senators actively involved. Partly for this reason, legislators have found it both feasible and congenial to ground their politics in systematic analyses of arms control questions.

Thus in recent years, many members who lack Congressman Aspin's professional background in systems analysis have performed key functions by drawing on analyses prepared by others. Personal preference and ideological inclination weigh substantially in congressional decisions on arms control, but increasingly those preferences and inclinations are molded by more or less thorough analysis of national security matters.

A principal factor in this developing linkage of arms control politics to arms control analyses is the shift in the composition of the Congress. As former Speaker of the House Carl Albert commented to his successor, Congressman Tip O'Neill, younger members of Congress "know how to use serious analysis and are demanding more of it." Later in the discussion we shall examine some of the analytic capabilities on which Congress has come to depend and consider some methods for enhancing their value.

For now, however, let us note that Congress, whether or not its politics has been informed by thorough analysis, has had an indisputable and major impact on many aspects of contemporary arms control. The entire history of the Strategic Arms Limitation Talks (SALT) is studded with congressional interventions. After the talks began sluggishly in 1969, the Senate attempted to prod them forward by a 1970 resolution urging a freeze on strategic offensive and defensive forces. Widespread skepticism in Congress helped to restrain administration proposals for deployment of Antiballistic Missile Systems. This go-slow approach afforded time for diplomacy to produce the ABM Treaty of 1972, requiring both the Soviet Union and the United States to severely limit ABM deployments. Subsequent negotiations were guided by the famous Jackson Amendment of 1972, in which Congress explicitly demanded that future agreements include the principle of equal ceilings for both sides. At the same time, in approving the Interim Agreement on Offensive Forces, Congress called for strategic arms reductions and exerted pressure on the executive branch not to be content merely with stabilizing stategic forces at high levels.

The impulse toward reductions accounted for the rather cool reception accorded the 1974 Vladivostok Accord between President Ford and Secretary Brezhnev. Many senators, ranging from Henry Jackson to Edward Kennedy, considered the Vladivostok ceilings of 2,400 strategic delivery vehicles (of which 1,320 could be MIRV launchers) excessive, and more likely to stimulate a build-up than to produce actual reductions. Equally significant, a number of legislators interpreted the original Vladivostok communique as implying that follow-on negotiations would be deferred for years. They pressed immediately for clarification on the point and, without formal action on any congressional resolution, prompted Moscow and Washington to commit themselves explicitly to prompt and continuing negotiations aimed at reducing deployments below the Valdivostok levels. It is widely assumed that congressional pressure contributed to President Carter's initial proposals to the Soviet Union that the two countries cut the Vladivostok ceilings by 17 to 25 percent, a range close to that suggested in 1974 by Senator Jackson.

The Senate in particular has used its diplomatic leverage potently to steer executive behavior on other arms control issues. When the Nixon administration submitted the Geneva Protocol on Chemical Weapons for ratification, half a century after the document had been drawn, the Foreign Relations Committee withheld action until satisfactory interpretations were forthcoming on a number of disputed provisions.[2] The primary disputes concerned the protocol's application to herbicides and so-called riot-control agents (RCAs). Herbicides had essentially been nonexistent when the protocol was drafted, but they had become controversial chemical agents during the Vietnam War, when they were used both to clear the perimeters of military bases and to defoliate large areas to deprive the enemy of cover. Similarly, though RCAs were available when the protocol was signed, they too had acquired novel usage during the war in Southeast Asia, when tear gas was occasionally used to flush combatants from shelter and thus expose them to artillery or aerial bombardment. International sentiment favored extending the protocol's interpretation to cover such uses in warfare, but, primarily to avoid *ex post facto* allegations of illegality, the executive branch resisted such interpretations while hostilities continued in Vietnam. As the war wound down, the Ford administration eventually yielded to international and senatorial demands and offered acceptable formulations of the protocol's relevance to the use of RCAs and herbicides.

A less conclusive episode involved the attempt to move beyond the partial nuclear test ban treaty of 1963. The Senate had facilitated that treaty by signaling its willingness to accept an accord covering those zones in which testing could be monitored adequately (under water, in the atmosphere, and in outer space), while deferring action on underground testing until such time as verification capabilities or on-site inspections would be sufficient to monitor compliance. By the 1970s sentiment in Congress had swung to support for a comprehensive ban, presumably even one relying on so-called national means of verification. Against the grain of those sentiments, the administration concluded in 1974 a Threshold Test Ban, followed some months later by a separate agreement on Peaceful Nuclear Explosions. Having signed the pacts, however, the administration chose not to press for ratification in the face of the Senate Foreign Relations Committee's evident reluctance to support the Threshold Test Ban. The legislative-executive standoff on this matter lingered into the Carter administration as a sore point for the Soviet Union, which complained repeatedly about American unwillingness to implement agreements it had signed. The incident was a vivid measure of congressional clout on arms control, reinforcing President Carter's interest in pursuing a comprehensive prohibition on tests.

More diffuse, but in some ways more suggestive, were the ways in which congressional forces converged on the problems of nuclear proliferation during the early 1970s. Seldom has an issue of such portent received so little attention in high levels of the government, although earlier efforts had produced the Non-Proliferation Treaty of 1963. This was as true in the Congress as in the executive branch. The principal legislative body dealing with nuclear matters, the Joint Committee on

Atomic Energy, persistently neglected the troubling dimensions of nuclear proliferation. Nevertheless, as the problem grew steadily more serious with the spread of nuclear power around the globe, other committees and other members of Congress began to seek a handle on the subject. Working from the Senate Committee on Banking, Housing, and Urban Affairs, Senator Adlai Stevenson came to grips with export control measures to curb the spread of nuclear technology with potential military applications. Senators Abraham Ribicoff, John Glenn, and William Brock used their service on the government Operations Committee to underscore the myriad aspects of the proliferation dilemma. In the House, Congressman Clement Zablocki tackled proliferation issues as chairman of the International Relations Subcommittee on International Security and Scientific Affairs.

The combined efforts of these and other legislators generated substantial, growing demand for a vigorous executive effort to cope with the prospect of nuclear proliferation. Indeed, the relative lethargy of the executive on these questions was overcome in considerable degree because of the climate of concern established and nourished by congressional critiques. It was that climate of anxiety which encouraged both presidential candidates in 1976 to frame unprecedented proposals to deal with proliferation.

Lessons and Legacies of the SALT Era

Recent experience in these and other cases underscores several continuing factors in the congressional approach to arms control. It also illustrates some of the problems Congress encounters in deploying its analytical and political resources on arms control issues.

First, for congressmen to be consistently effective on complex questions of arms control, they must have multiple avenues of access to information and influence on such questions. Obviously there is an institutional trade-off between the dangers of relying on a closed loop in which one or two committees and a small number of congressmen have a virtual monopoly on an issue, and the hazards of excessive fragmentation in which numerous committees and legislators jockey for positions of authority over a given problem. At considerable cost to the coherence and tautness of its organizational arrangements, Congress has increasingly opted for redundancy in treating arms control subjects. Such redundancy is especially important with issues that invite the practice of secrecy and other constraints on information which at once amplify the power of insiders and intimidate outsiders from expressing judgments. In earlier years these influences produced disproportionate leverage on national security and arms control matters for the Armed Services Committees in both houses, as well as the Joint Committee on Atomic Energy, all of which attained a state of relative imperviousness to the opinions and perspectives of those outside the closed information exchange with the national security bureaucracy.

Disillusionment with the modern performance of the principal national security committees largely accounts for widespread resistance in Congress to the recurring proposal to create a joint committee on national security.[3] In the recent Senate reform of its committee structure, the idea of consolidating the authority of the Foreign Relations and Armed Services Committees into a single committee on national security was quickly abandoned. Furthermore, both the House and the Senate have moved to abandon the joint committee form in several cases, notably by abolishing the Joint Committee on Atomic Energy. These developments reflect a general appreciation that, while national security issues require discretion and high responsibility, restricting access and concentrating power to deal with them are counterproductive.

A second continuing factor is the propensity of the executive branch to manipulate the congressional handling of arms control issues. A classic instance, perhaps based on inadequate preparation by the Defense Department, was Secretary James Schlesinger's attempt to persuade the Senate Subcommittee on Arms Control that counterforce attacks against American military installations would generate relatively few casualties, which he estimated as several hundred thousand.[4] Senator Clifford Case, dismayed by the "whole razzle dazzle" of the calculations presented, pressed for more refined analyses of the casualties and destruction likely to result from counterforce attacks in the continental United States.

Analysis of the most selective sort marked the entire Defense Department performance as it attempted to fend off the senator's criticism of its initial projections. Its initial response to Case's challenge was to invoke a 1968 Senate Armed Services Subcommittee report that seemed to support a U.S. counterforce capability, while ignoring subsequent committee actions that specifically restrained U.S. counterforce technology. Gradually and grudgingly, in the face of independent analyses prepared for Congress by the Office of Technology Assessment (OTA) and others, Secretary Schlesinger acknowledged that the plausible casualty range for a major counterforce attack against the United States was much higher than the one he initially had given. Whether the department's performance constituted deliberate deception or mere incompetence, the dispute over counterforce strikes and limited war confirmed the need for congressional wariness toward self-serving executive presentations regarding arms control and military strategy.

The third and most emphatic lesson of the last decade is that early penetration of arms control issues is the key to congressional success in coping with them. This requires a far different attitude than the traditional congressional stance of awaiting executive formulations before launching study and action. Increasingly, individual legislators and committees are seeking to identify emerging arms control questions in time to participate, at least indirectly, in the bureaucratic process of shaping the issues for decision. The velocity and volume of public policy issues are simply too great for Congress to function according to the Schattschneider maxim that "The President proposes, the Congress disposes."

Members of Congress have been groping extensively for improved early warning of impending arms control problems. Among the formal devices they have instituted, the so-called arms control impact statement and arrangements for prior reports of foreign military sales are outstanding examples. Unfortunately, the results of both procedures have so far been quite mixed.

During 1976 the Department of Defense and the Energy Research and Development Administration (ERDA) submitted their first arms control impact statements regarding sixteen separate programs. Although submitted on a classified basis, the statements were neither responsive nor adequately detailed. As John Sparkman, chairman of the Foreign Relations Committee, told the Senate, "We concluded that the arms control impact statements submitted by the Department and by ERDA do not comply with the law and are unacceptable, and we asked that they resubmit comprehensive statements on the programs covered by the initial submissions."[5] The statements, he said, were simply too late, too brief, and too insubstantial to be useful to anyone with a passing familiarity with the programs. Sparkman's speech followed an independent critique of the impact statements by Charles Gellner of the Congressional Research Service. As eventually made available on an unclassified basis, the Defense Department's statements can only be described as embarrassingly bad. Although the first round of arms control impact statements thus produced more evasion than good-faith compliance, Senators Humphrey, Case, and others pledged themselves to pursue the executive branch diligently in demanding further reports on the arms control implications of proposed weapons systems.

In assuming direction of ACDA, Paul Warnke pledged fuller compliance with the impact statement procedure. Yet during the controversy over "enhanced radiation weapons" in the summer of 1977, a major complaint of the weapons' opponents was that neither the Ford nor the Carter administration had followed the law in this regard. The belated submission of an impact statement on these weapons to the president and subsequently to Congress represented some improvement, but still smacked of haste and inadequate review. The episode suggested that friction would persist between the branches unless more creditable impact analyses were forthcoming on proposed weapons programs.

If the arms control impact statement generated disappointingly skimpy information, the reporting requirements on foreign military sales, intended to permit Congress to consider potentially provocative sales of American weaponry before they are consummated, may have produced an unmanageable overload. Late in the 94th Congress, having withheld reports on prospective military sales until the last moment, the Ford administration dumped on Congress a large number of such reports involving many millions of dollars. Although a few transactions such as the proposed sale of Hawk missiles to Jordan and other transfers to the volatile Middle East had received substantial legislative review, the manner of executive reporting defeated the purpose of the requirement. Off the record, executive officials admitted that the military sales reports were presented in a way intended to frustrate congressional intervention.

Clearly, Congress must refine these procedures if they are to bear fruit. Executive conduct in these cases bred well-justified outrage on Capitol Hill. Yet, properly coordinated, these and similar procedures should contribute to constructive and timely legislative action.

Given the rampant decentralization of Congress, it seems likely that the most frequent routes toward early congressional involvement in arms control questions will be those marked out by individual legislators aggressively searching out problems that interest and concern them. This often requires individual congressmen and senators to play on the bureaucracy's turf, seeking to catalyze executive action, to highlight congressional interests, and occasionally to protect "whistle-blowers" who have alerted Congress to items of special significance. It will be difficult to balance the need for a degree of legislative intrusiveness with the need for coherent executive authority, but the tension between these values cannot be resolved satisfactorily by admonishing congressmen to stay out of the bureaucracy's business.

How valuable the initiative of individual congressmen can be is demonstrated by the history of the nuclear proliferation question. Amid much anxiety but little action, the proliferation problem languished in the executive branch for years. The situation in Congress was little better until the Senate turned its attention to the Energy Re-organization Act of 1974. Work on that legislation led Senator Abraham Ribicoff of the Government Operations Committee and his staff assistant Paul Leventhal to examine closely nuclear exports and related activities.[6] As an observer at the Non-Proliferation Treaty Review Conference of May 1975, Leventhal found himself increasingly persuaded that nuclear safeguards posed a severe problem and that commercial considerations were distorting policy on nuclear exports. Subsequently, Ribicoff became an animated leader of the campaign to revise U.S. policy, and his vocal initiatives helped to spur new policies in both the Ford and Carter administrations. Of course the senator had many allies in both houses, but the evolution of the nuclear export control issue probably owes more to him than to any other legislator. His experience confirms once more that congressional effectiveness often depends on the determination and perseverance of an individual legislator committed to a great issue.

New Resources and an Attentive Network

Among the reasons to hope that Congress will sustain its interest in arms control and improve its capacity to act in this field is the development of an attentive network that now links members and committees of Congress with able policy analysts in the central staffs of Congress and in the private sector. In and around Congress a considerable number of antennae are now attuned to arms control issues. In addition to its direct engagement on matters of defense budgeting, the Congressional Budget Office has begun to provide significant analyses of such questions as the relationship of the strategic forces budget to the Strategic Arms Limitation Talks.[7] The Budget Office staff has also produced a series of studies concerned with American general purpose forces. One can expect a continuing flow of analyses germane to arms control as the Budget Office continues to explore ways to make its studies more useful to members of Congress and their staffs.

Other central staffs have also improved their contributions to arms control deliberations. The General Accounting Office has offered creditable assessments of the functions and potential of the International Atomic Energy Agency (IAEA) in implementing and enforcing safeguards. In addition, it provided a major critique of the cost-benefit analyses involved in the Ford administration's proposal to turn over to private industry portions of the nation's uranium-enrichment capability. The Congressional Research Service has published work on the Soviet-American military balance, as well as studies of various environmental and proliferation problems relevant to arms control.[8] Although the Office of Technology Assessment has generally shunned national security problems, its notable work on the consequences of limited nuclear war, already mentioned, has been followed by a substantial volume on nuclear proliferation and safeguards.[9]

Congress is also benefiting from the effort of private participants in the arms control community. The Council for a Livable World has long concentrated its attention in this field, working closely with senators and congressmen to whose campaigns the Council sometimes contributes. Of a different order are the relations to Congress of groups like the Arms Control Association and the Federation of American Scientists. Their publications have found a wide audience in the House and Senate, and when asked for help, such groups frequently mobilize expert witnesses to assist committees in developing testimony on arms control.[10]

Creation of this attentive network, and especially its extension to independent private organizations and analysts, has structured a tighter grid in which significant issues for arms control may be examined. It is less and less likely that important arms control questions will simply not come to the attention of Congress. A growing number of congressmen and their associates now have a stake in seeing that Congress performs the functions outlined at the beginning of this chapter. This does not guarantee sound decisions, but it reduces the probability that significant arms control issues will escape legislative scrutiny altogether. The neutron bomb case, however, is a sharp reminder that the weapons development and procurement process can still present congressmen—and presidents—with *faits accomplis.*

Nevertheless, Congress needs to make further major improvements in its approach to arms control. Random interventions in matters as complex as arms control may also be reckless ones, and this is a perpetual hazard in how Congress currently approaches these problems. Now that the legislature has shifted from a passive to an active stance, it becomes all the more essential that it act rationally, after prudently assessing the consequences of its decisions. Thus, we inevitably return to the perennial dilemmas of relating political behavior to systematic analysis of policy options.

Three Areas for Improvement

Enhancing Congress's capacity to deal sensitively in this area will require progress on three principal fronts: (1) better access to information; (2) new modes of analysis; and (3) more refined definition of the level and scope of congressional action—all examined below.

1. Congress is deluged with information, yet much of it is too disorganized or disconnected to be useful. In addition to the vast expansion of their own paper-generating capacity, members and staffs have grown highly sophisticated in tapping the bureaucracy for data and reports. Nevertheless, the results remain generally mixed and frequently unsatisfactory. One approach to providing a common data base between the legislative and executive branches, so far as national security issues are concerned, was advanced by Senator John Sherman Cooper before his retirement. Senator Cooper proposed that the appropriate committees of Congress have access to the findings of the intelligence community and to National Security Council studies. These intelligence estimates and study memoranda, the senator correctly pointed out, consolidate assessments of facts and options for public policy. Without violating the privileged nature of his subordinates' recommendations, the president could package and share with authorized members and committees of Congress under suitable classification and controls the basic data and analyses on which presidential decisions presumably rest. The Cooper plan remains a candidate for serious consideration, and indeed it has been implemented in a fragmentary way. The Senate Intelligence Committee reportedly has good access to intelligence findings, although other committees remain vulnerable to selective disclosure designed to support executive recom-

mendations rather than to equip Congress for independent policy formulation. The resolution creating the Intelligence Committee is noteworthy for its assertion of the committee's right not only to obtain intelligence reports, but, on appeal to the Senate, even to release classified information without the president's approval if the Senate deems it essential for the public to have the information.[11] The House has now created a parallel committee on virtually identical lines.

In testimony before the House International Relations Committee, I proposed a more far-reaching concept for facilitating and systematizing congressional access to classified information.[12] This plan calls for a congressional agent to be designated the Foreign Policy Auditor and modeled on the Comptroller General. The Foreign Policy Auditor would be responsible for striking a balance between the need for independent legislative evaluation of intelligence and high-level policy analyses and the evident risks of widely circulating sensitive information among congressional offices.

Properly cleared and subjected to the standard governance of the classification system, the Foreign Policy Auditor and his small staff would perform three functions for Congress. First, on behalf of the majority and minority leaders of the House and Senate, the auditor would monitor intelligence and National Security Council analyses, as well as other interdepartmental analyses on which policy is to be grounded. On the basis of such monitoring, congressional leaders and, under their direction, other appropriate congressmen would be advised of emerging issues on which they might wish to intervene. Second, if asked by the executive branch, the auditor could offer opinions regarding questions arising in the intelligence analyses on which the president wished congressional counsel. Third, and probably of greatest importance, the auditor would brief the congressional leaders and other members they designated before major consultations with the executive branch. This would help redress a central failing of present arrangements for consultation between the branches. Such encounters are demonstrably less useful than they might be because, more often than not, the congressional participants are inadequately prepared for independent appraisal of the rationales and arguments presented by the executive.

There is no ideal solution to the information access problem. It is imperative, however, for Congress to continue experimenting with formal and informal mechanisms to improve its access to relevant data and analyses. On arms control and other foreign policy matters, a common data base subjected to separate evaluations by the legislative and executive branches could go far toward forging a common view of controversial issues. Conversely, a healthy legislative-executive alliance is harder to forge when congressmen feel they are exploited, snowed, and manipulated by executive monopoly of the relevant information.

2. Despite the plethora of staffs and documents circulating in Congress, there is ample room for innovation in the modes of policy analysis employed there. Mechanisms for evaluating information and for focusing it on the needs of harried members are not so much lacking as poorly deployed and directed. Whether one is speaking of arms control or of other complexities, the modes of analysis that should ideally be available to congressmen are those which ensure that studies are actually used.

There is no question that congressional staffs have been upgraded in recent years; although the record is uneven, the quality of the studies they produce is demonstrably superior to that which prevailed a decade ago. Yet members continue to complain about the blandness of congressional staff reports. Here congressmen are victims of their own divided impulses. They want candid assessments by competent professionals, and at the same time they ask for options only, lest their own decision-making prerogatives fall prey to "expert" opinion. Even the excellent reports of the Congressional Budget Office eschew explicit recommendations, although the presentation of policy options has been unusually trenchant. In many other cases staff reports are poorly written and sometimes pretentious; in 1975 one fifty-page report was accompanied by a sixteen-page index.

At the same time there is a justifiable complaint among most central staffs of Congress that members tend to ignore even outstanding work. This basically reflects the pressures on

members' time and not the quality of staff analyses, but the
effects are the same: demoralized analytic staffs and prolonged
distress among members who feel poorly served. Evidently
there is a fundamental challenge to shape staff reports so that
they capture members' attention and satisfy the needs they
perceive.

At a general level one can describe the requirements for
meeting this challenge. Analyses should be constructed in ways
that relate to the members' political interests, either in terms of
their standing within Congress and with their constituents, or
in terms of their policy emphases. A promising means of
exciting interest in members is to engage them at the outset, so
far as feasible, in identifying and formulating the issues for
analysis. This gives them a stake in the outcome, thus
increasing the chances both that the material will be relevant to
their needs and that they will be aroused to act upon it when the
studies finally emerge. Another useful stratagem would be to
harness the competitive instincts of members and committees
by identifying and studying problems that cut across committee jurisdictions. Nothing attracts a member's attention
more effectively than the prospect that a competing committee
will seize a lively issue and make a successful run with
it.

With varying degrees of intensity and consistency, the
analytic staffs of Congress have attempted to reach these goals.
In most cases they face severe obstacles—for example, in the
strong proprietary claims of individual members and committees who commission particular studies. The General Accounting Office and other agencies have frequently been barred
from reporting results to a particular committee because the
work had been performed for another committee, which
forbade wider distribution of the report.[13] Even the Office of
Technology Assessment, which is governed by a board linking
the interests of numerous committees in both houses, has found
itself responding primarily to requests by individual committees, although its work has been generally available to the
membership as a whole. The central agencies of Congress
would do well to initiate more cross-cutting studies on their
own authority.[14]

In addition, and here the OTA holds much promise, Congress must develop the capacity to contract for analyses, especially in such arcane fields as arms control. By tapping private resources, Congress can both diversify the analytic capabilities at its disposal and slow the massive expansion of the legislative bureaucracy by using short-term, project-oriented staffs in the private sector. Meeting this goal, however, will require marked changes in the organization of Congress's committees and central agencies in order to engage and manage contractors. Equally vital is developing congressionally oriented institutions in the private sector that can supply trustworthy and professional analyses for Congress. By design and practice the Office of Technology Assessment has geared its efforts in this direction.

Whether Congress resorts to wider use of contract analyses, it can at least adapt its present analytic formats to overcome their most glaring weaknesses. In fact, sophisticated reform of the study formats could help offset the admitted decline in the quality of legislative debate. A commendable approach might be described as analytic debate or adversary analysis. This concept would use analytic teams incorporating not only the broadest range of relevant disciplines but a range of perspectives and policy preferences as well. In each case the study could be conducted by a group of analysts deliberately selected both for their technical competence and for their known divergence of opinions. For example, to evaluate future strategic force options one might wish to assemble a team of distinguished analysts like Thomas Schelling, Albert Wohl-stetter, and George Rathjens. Under suitable auspices such a group could compose an analytic debate consisting of three main sections.

In section one the analysts would be constrained to formulate a unanimous statement of the data: what do we know and agree upon as the basic facts relevant to this problem? They would, of course, retain the right to annotate disagreements and to identify facts in dispute. In section two the analysts would prepare a joint statement of the options for public action: what is the range of realistic policy choices that Congress should consider? In section three, however, the debate format would liberate the individual analyst. Each would be encouraged to formulate individual or joint rationales for particular options: what should the nation do? In this manner the study normally would produce not one conclusion, but several, unless there were an unusual convergence of judgment on a particular issue.

Political scientists will recognize the kinship between this proposed technique for analytic debate and the idea of multiple advocacy in policy making which Alexander George advanced some years ago.[15] A structured procedure for analytic debate, coupled with arrangements for internal critiques by the study teams and external critiques by professionals not associated with them, could in principle produce unusually refined and systematic material for policymakers. Since issues of the magnitude of arms control generally have extended half-lives, there should be no pretense that a single exercise in adversary analysis is sufficient or conclusive. Rather, it should be conceived as part of a continuing, open-ended process in which newer and potentially more useful options might emerge from the analysis and be subjected to further evaluation. A cardinal advantage of embedding analysts of diverse skills and views in the procedure is that it helps simultaneously to hone their analyses and to keep the participants honest about their preferences.

From the standpoint of congressional users, many of whom have commented on this model, the analytic-debate concept holds significant promise. In reading most so-called options papers, congressmen always face the problem of figuring out where the authors stand. Has some hidden preference led the writer, even unintentionally, to manipulate the reader? By obliging the analysts to make explicit their own preferences, analytic debates can help assure congressmen and their staffs that they are not confronting a snow job. By skipping to the back of the book, as it were, the readers can find out where the authors stand. They can then ask, did the analysts skew the data to favor one outcome over the others? Were the options fairly presented, or subtly distorted to guide the reader in a particular direction. In other words, section three of the proposed analyses would equip the congressional reader to judge the competence and balance of the first sections more confidently.

It would be naive to expect every member of Congress to act solely on the basis of sound analysis. Some members will choose their course of action on other bases, possibly before ever examining such a study. Yet the existence of multiple rationales in an analytic debate can help members present the most systematic case for their preferred option, however they may have chosen it. Thus, both for those seeking help in resolving complex dilemmas and for those whose political stands are already established, analytic debates of this nature could perform a distinct service. They could provide the model for work either in the existing central staffs of Congress or, more probably, on the part of carefully selected contractors. No other mode of analysis seems so responsive to the pluralistic character of legislative decision making.

3. However good its access to information and however sophisticated its analysis of arms control issues, Congress will still find difficulties in identifying the suitable level on which to act. There is a ramshackle quality to some congressional interventions in arms control; members persist in groping for the best handles on such topics. Should Congress attempt to formulate the basic ingredients of a complex strategic doctrine? Should it focus on particular weapons systems and try to evaluate the comparative advantages of one weapon over another? Should it instead limit itself to budgetary guidance, setting dollar ceilings within which the national security establishment must operate? By what means and at what points in an extended international negotiation should Congress seek to participate?

One might begin to answer those questions by asking some others. Would arms control have benefited most if Senator Ribicoff had not investigated details of export practices on nuclear technology and had not severely criticized sales practices of Germany, France, and other allies? Would arms control objectives have been well served if Congressman Zablocki and Senator Edward Brooke had not interfered in the development and deployment of MIRV warhead systems? Could legislators have intervened more effectively in the MIRV case if they had known more about the state of the negotiations?

Would American strategic doctrine, still afflicted with many internal contradictions, have evolved more constructively if Senator Case had taken no interest in retargeting American strategic forces under Secretary of Defense Schlesinger? Would the Carter administration have shown such acute concern for the lavish transfers of conventional arms if Senator Humphrey and others had not begun to tighten congressional approval of such transactions?

As these counterquestions suggest, there is strong evidence that the relative disorderliness of congressional involvement in arms control has a real value of its own. Congress is a collection of individual policy entrepreneurs, and one of its great virtues is that each of them may perceive and advertise significant issues for decision, though none of them possesses the power of final action. Personally, I would favor no rule that sought to impede the possibility of congressional action on any level. From the trivial to the cosmic, no issue should be excluded from Congress's political radar, which frequently, just by detecting and reporting a problem, can help to trigger needed action.

Nevertheless, there remains a tremendous burden on Congress as an institution to shape coherent action on the more important questions and to avoid distraction by the less important. A cardinal challenge for congressional leadership, supported by responsible executive persuasion, will be to guide Congress toward a sensible selection of legislative priorities. The institution is so vulnerable to overload on the one hand and to divide-and-conquer strategy on the other that it cannot expect laissez-faire procedures to suffice.

Several innovations in recent years demonstrate that Congress can find an appropriate level from which to act responsibly. The War Powers Act and, even more significant, the budget reform of 1974 strike a prudent balance between executive initiative and orderly legislative determination of high policy. In the arms control area specifically, refining the impact statement can produce for Congress structured, more informed opportunities for decision, through systematic and comparative presentations of the necessary information.

Although the dozens of legislative veto opportunities now

on the books approach the maximum desirable number, such mechanisms permit Congress potential for action without requiring it to intercede in every instance. This is particularly the case in areas like conventional arms transfers, where only occasionally and intermittently will Congress have sufficient grasp of the details of a particular situation to warrant a judgment separate from that of the executive.[16] Congress should not, however, tolerate an executive attitude that seeks to deal with Congress by deluging it with detailed reports beyond the legislature's capacity to absorb or assess. To sustain its capacity for meaningful review, Congress must insist that the executive branch phase its reports in a manageable flow, rather than concentrating large numbers of them late in the fiscal year. Progress in this direction is already evident, but Congress will have to discipline itself not only to obtain the reports but to ensure thorough staff evaluations of them.

On balance, there appears to be no clear solution to the level-of-action problem. Arms control policy and a healthy legislative-executive relationship both require further improvement in Congress's institutional mechanisms for action in this field, as well as continued tolerance for the myriad efforts of individual legislators on a host of complex problems. The record to date is very mixed, but congressional contribution to arms control policy has been indisputably positive and is expanding. The Capitol remains the home of both skeptics and advocates of arms control as an instrument of national security policy. And in their contest for leadership, members of Congress give the electorate its best opportunity to influence which risks America will choose in world affairs.

Notes

1. See Alton Frye, "Congressional Politics and Policy Analysis: Bridging the Gap," *Policy Analysis* 2 (Spring 1976): 265-81.

2. U.S., Congress, Senate, Committee on Foreign Relations, *Prohibition of Chemical and Biological Weapons* (hearing), 93rd Cong., 2d sess., December 10, 1974.

3. An interesting reflection of this sentiment is found in the congressional survey reported as Appendix M of the *Report of the Commission on the Organization of the Government for the Conduct*

of Foreign Policy 5 (June 1975): 119-36.

4. U.S., Congress, Senate, Subcommittee on Arms Control, International Law, and Organization of the Committee on Foreign Relations, *Briefing on Counterforce Attacks* (hearing), 93rd Cong., 2d sess., September 11, 1974 ("sanitized" and made public on January 10, 1975). A definitive review of this case is found in Sidney D. Drell and Frank von Hippel, "Limited Nuclear War," *Scientific American* 235 (November 1976): 27-37.

5. *Congressional Record*, September 17, 1976, S-16096-100.

6. See Abraham A. Ribicoff, "A Market Sharing Approach to the Nuclear Sales Problem," *Foreign Affairs* 54 (July 1976): 763-87. Senator John Glenn's work also deserves special note in this connection. See his statement, "The Safety and Security of Our Nuclear Exports," *Congressional Record*, February 18, 1976, S-1800-806.

7. For example, see *U.S. Strategic Nuclear Forces: Deterrence Policies and Procurement Issues,* Congressional Budget Office, April 1977. Also see *SALT and the U.S. Strategic Forces Budget,* Congressional Budget Office, Background Paper no. 8, June 23, 1976.

8. *United States/Soviet Military Balance: A Frame of Reference for Congress,* Library of Congress Congressional Research Service, January 1976.

9. *Nuclear Proliferation and Safeguards,* Office of Technology Assessment, April 1977.

10. Notable examples of the work of the Federation of American Scientists Association are "Proliferation," *F. A. S. Public Interest Report,* October 1976; and Congressman Les Aspin, "Soviet Civil Defense: Myth and Reality," *Arms Control Today,* September 1976.

11. See Section 8 of Senate Resolution 400, March 1, 1976.

12. U.S., Congress, House, Special Subcommittee on Investigations of the Committee on International Relations, *Congress and Foreign Policy* (hearing), 94th Cong., 2d sess., June 17, 1976, pp. 12-54.

13. Consider the exchange between Comptroller General Elmer Staats and Congressman Benjamin Rosenthal in U.S., Congress, House, *Review of the Powers, Procedures, and Policies of the General Accounting Office* (hearing), the Committee on Government Operations, Subcommittee of 94th Cong., 1st sess., December 10, 1975, pp. 14-17.

14. This was a major point of the Commission on the Operation of the Senate in its *Interim Report,* 94th Cong., 2d sess., March 31, 1976, Senate Doc. 94-165, p. 10.

15. See Alexander L. George, "The Case for Multiple Advocacy

in Making Foreign Policy," *American Political Science Review* 66 (September 1972): 751-95, including a comment by I. M. Destler and a rejoinder by the author.

16. See Leslie H. Gelb, "Arms Sales," *Foreign Policy* 25 (Winter 1976-77): 3-23.

3
The Power of Procedure

Les Aspin

It is an article of faith among politicians and political scientists that Congress possesses ultimate control over executive actions because "Congress controls the purse strings." When it comes to arms, however, the power of the purse often turns out to be a sham.

Congress rarely adds or subtracts a major new weapons system in votes on the floor. This results partly from lack of time but mainly from lack of expertise among members of Congress. Most congressmen serve on committees that deal with matters other than defense. They worry about health issues, welfare problems, or economy, and think about defense matters twice a year, when the military authorization and appropriation bills reach the floor. It is difficult for these congressmen to say no if the executive branch, with all its military and civilian expertise massed behind it, says the country must have a particular weapons system.

This is not to say there are no congressmen who will take the lead and oppose the Pentagon. There are several, but they come from the thin ranks of those who specialize in defense. It is exceptional if they can persuade a majority of the House and Senate to differ with the administration on a major weapons system.

This is a judgment borne out by history. No major weapon has ever been defeated in either house. The closest call was the 1969 vote on the Antiballistic Missile (ABM). The effort to kill the ABM failed on a tie vote in the Senate. It is easy to forget what a unique political event the ABM debate was. Several influences converged: the arms control community argued that the ABM would not work, and numerous spokesmen for it were ready to come to Washington to explain to congressmen why it would not; peace groups said the ABM was destabilizing and were concerned enough to lobby intensely; hostile constituent pressure (almost unheard-of on a weapons system issue) was brought to bear by people living near proposed ABM sites; and, finally, the weapon was not then in production, so that members of Congress did not face pressures from large numbers of workers fearful of losing their jobs. The ABM controversy brought together a constellation of forces that is not likely to be repeated by chance and is almost impossible to put together by design.

Opponents of the B-1 were never able to marshal all these forces. It is worth noting that only two days before President Carter decided to kill the bomber, the House voted 243-178 to support it. And even after Carter came out against the B-1, the House sustained his position by the narrow margin of 202-199. Even with the administration opposed to the B-1, that weapon had sufficient appeal (not to mention backing from business and labor groups) to come within three votes of a majority.

Congress actually does very little to pare the defense requests of any administration. I recently had the Library of Congress review the actions of Congress on the defense budgets for the six fiscal years from 1971 through 1976—years when antidefense feelings in the country were at their peak, and Congress and the executive branch were controlled by different parties. The total dollar reductions imposed on the Defense Department came to 6.3 percent of the cumulative requests. The study then analyzed the kinds of reductions that were made and found:

1. Nine percent of the cuts were in *noncritical* areas such as reductions in servants for generals, in the number of public relations men at the Pentagon, and in funds for the construction of new commissaries.
2. Thirty-five percent were *illusory* cuts or simply financial adjustments, such as the elimination of aid for South

Vietnam after Saigon had fallen and of funds that the services had testified were no longer needed because of changed circumstances.

3. Twenty percent were not cuts but *postponements;* for example, if a program was experiencing development difficulties, Congress dropped funds for procurement until the problems were resolved.

4. The remaining 36 percent of the cuts (or just 2 percent of the total requests) were in areas that could actually affect defense policy.

However, as the library pointed out, even this overstated the substantive reductions: "For instance, the elimination of a weapon system is always treated as substantive rather than non-critical even if the system is in fact ineffective, duplicative of other systems, etc." The study concludes that congressional reductions in the Defense budget between Fiscal Year 1971 and Fiscal Year 1976 were "less critical than might be supposed by a superficial presentation of the total reductions. . . . Congress has exercised only a limited influence on U.S. policy and the military force structure."

What limited budget impact Congress has had comes from the defense-related committees. When defense appropriations bills come to the floor, the House and Senate normally do little more than tinker with them. In the last two decades the House has cut a net of only .04 percent from the appropriations bills brought before it. The Senate has cut only .06 percent. And in half those years floor action in one house or the other made no change whatsoever in the sums appropriated for defense.

Whereas Congress as a whole lacks the expertise to defy the weapons lobby, the defense committees—the two Armed Services Committees and the two Defense Appropriations Subcommittees—do not have that problem. They are hobbled, however, by constituent interest.

When congressmen are elected, one of their first priorities is to ensure their reelection. Chances for reelection are not enhanced by concentrating on national legislation. Junior members—and to a large extent senior members as well—are reelected on the basis of what they do for their constituents.

This involves both the smaller chores, like resolving Social Security problems for senior citizens, and the larger economic concerns of the community they represent, such as arranging federal financing for a new dam.

Congressmen elected from districts with special economic interests are likely to gravitate to committees that have some influence over those interests. A congressman from the wheat belt will try to get on the Agriculture Committee; one from a fishing port will want a seat on Merchant Marine and Fisheries; and the congressman from Cape Canaveral will want to be on the Science and Technology Committee. Congressmen from areas with major military bases or defense industries usually turn up on the Armed Services Committee. It is not by coincidence that of the representatives from the Norfolk, Virginia, area—home of the largest naval complex on the East Coast—all three serve on the House Armed Services Committee. Also on the committee is a congressman from the San Diego area, which has the largest concentration of military personnel in the country, and one from the San Antonio area, with the major concentration of Air Force personnel. The largest Marine base is at Camp LeJeune, North Carolina, and the congressman representing that district also serves on the committee. Although the largest Army base is Fort Hood, Texas, no congressman from that area is on the committee. The Army suffers, in fact from a severe underrepresentation; only one of its five biggest bases is represented.

Preference for specific committees is based not only on economics, but also on ideology. Conservatives concerned with national security tend to think in terms of military solutions and therefore seek seats on the Armed Services Committee, whereas liberals with international concerns gravitate to the International Relations Committee.

There is one further problem. Although it is not generally realized, the Armed Services Committees authorize only about one-third of the defense budget, mostly in procurement, research and development, and military construction. (The other two-thirds go mainly for manpower and day-to-day needs such as fuel and utilities.) Indeed, when the Armed Services Committees were formed in 1947, the only part of the defense budget they specifically authorized was that for military construction (about 3 percent of the total). Since 1961 the Armed Services Committees in both houses have extended their authority, first to procurement, then to research and development. And it is likely that their authority will gradually be extended in the years to come.

As a result of this historical development, members of the Armed Services Committees tend to define their job not in terms of overseeing the defense budget *per se*, but rather in closely scutinizing parts of it. Absorbed in minutiae, most members of the committees do not consider alternatives to proposed weapons because they simply do not regard themselves as responsible for the budget and defense program as a whole.

Therefore, the power of the purse is not the key to decisive congressional influence on arms control or weapons procurement. If we want Congress to act constructively, we must find another approach.

If there is one word that describes the essence of Congress, that word is "procedure." Congressmen love procedure, perhaps because many of them are lawyers. "Closed rules," "open rules," "motions to table," "consent calendars," "union calendars"—this is the stuff of which congressional decisions are made.

To understand the congressman's penchant for procedure, one must understand how it benefits him. In the first place, procedure allows Congress to construct a majority and to make progress. In an institution with many factions, at times one of the few things members can agree on is the procedure for resolving an issue. So, very often procedure becomes a substitute for substance.

Second, procedure allows congressmen to mask many of their votes from their constituents. The first end-the-Vietnam-War vote in the House of Representatives, for example, came on a motion to table a motion to instruct the conferees to insist on the House version of the Defense Authorization Bill in the light of the Legislative Reorganization Act of 1970. A congressman could vote as he chose and leave his constituents scratching their heads.

Every profession has devices to keep kibitzers and amateurs at arm's length. Procedure does that for Congress. When confronted by a constituent demanding explanation of a vote against funding for the B-1 bomber, the congressman can always say, "Well, it was brought up under a closed rule and that, of course, is just intolerable because it prevented a full and fair debate. We couldn't vote for it under those circumstances." He has the advantage, for although the constituent may know more about the bombers—the congressman knows more about closed rules.

Third, procedure allows Congress to defy the executive without confronting executive branch expertise. In 1972, for example, after the SALT agreement was signed, Defense Secretary Melvin R. Laird presented to the House and Senate Armed Services Committees recommendations for budget additions resulting from SALT. One of the items in Laird's budget was more money for the Hard-Target Re-entry Vehicle (HTRV), which faced heavy opposition in the Senate. The House Armed Services Committee was reconvened and the SALT additions approved. The Senate Armed Services Committee, however, decreed that the request had arrived too late for hearings and dropped the HTRV from the bill. When the conference committee met to iron out the differences between the two versions, the HTRV was rejected—not on the merits of the case (even though the principal people involved understood the issue), but on the procedural ground that only one house had considered the matter.

An incident described by David Halberstam in *The Best and the Brightest* (New York: Random House, 1973, pp. 140-141) illustrates the congressional instinct to avoid direct confrontation with the executive and achieve objectives through procedure. The incident concerned the American decision not to intervene in Indochina on behalf of the French in 1954.

On April 3, 1954, at Eisenhower's suggestion, Dulles met with the Congressional leadership, a group which included Minority Leader Lyndon B. Johnson and the ranking Democrat on the Armed Services Committee, Richard Russell.

The purpose of the meeting soon became clear: the Administration wanted a congressional resolution to permit the President to use naval and air power in Indochina, particularly a massive air strike to save the garrison at Dienbienphu. . . .

The senators began to question Radford. Would this be an act of war? Yes, we would be in the war. What would happen if the first air strike did not succeed in relieving the garrison? We would follow it up. What about ground forces? Radford gave an ambivalent answer. . . .

At this point Johnson took over. . . . Johnson was disturbed by the implications of the Radford appeal for a variety of reasons. He doubted that the necessary resources existed in a war-weary country which had just come out of Korea, and he did not want the blame for refusing to go to war placed on him and the Democratic leadership in Congress. If Eisenhower went for a congressional resolution, then Johnson would be right smack on the spot, which was exactly where he did not want to be. . . .

The Democrats, he told Dulles, had been blamed for the Korean War and for having gone in virtually alone without significant allies. . . . The patriotism of Democratic officials had been questioned. He was touched now to be considered so worthy and so good a patriot as to be requested to get on board. But first he had some questions. . . .What allies did they have who would put up sizeable amounts of men for Indochina? Had Dulles consulted with any allies? No, said the Secretary, he had not.

By the time the two-hour meeting was over, Johnson had exposed the frailty of the Administration's position. . . . Dulles was told to sign up allies. . . .Thus the burden, which the Administration had ever so gently been trying to shift to the Congress, had now been ever so gently shifted back, if not to the Administration, at least to the British, who were known to be unenthusiastic.

Procedure, then, can be and is used by Congress to avoid direct responsibility. Congressmen have recourse to procedure not only to mask their votes and achieve objectives without confronting the executive, but also to protect themselves politically. Congress as an institution does not like to be out front.

The decisive votes on a multibillion-dollar defense budget, which contains money for such diverse items as Safeguard

missile sites, a naval base at Diego Garcia, and military support
for the government of South Vietnam, will most likely be held
on nominally procedural questions, such as thresholds,
ceilings, and cut-off dates. The most capable legislators
understand this, perhaps instinctively. Congress establishes
thresholds which require, for example, that when x happens,
then y must happen; when a certain point is reached, then the
president must report to Congress (the War Powers Bill is an
example). Congress establishes ceilings requiring, for instance,
that spending for certain functions cannot exceed a specified
amount ($2.5 billion for Military Assistance Service Funded, or
$500 million for Transfer Authority). And Congress establishes
cut-off dates (e. g., the flight pay for colonels and generals who
do not fly stops May 31, or the bombing of Cambodia ends
August 15). Congressmen are most comfortable dealing with
national security matters in procedural terms; there they are the
experts.

All this may be discouraging to those who look to Congress
as a source of leadership. Very often such people think that if
Congress could get more information or reform in some way, it
would assume a leadership role. But the problem is not
information. In many ways Congress now has more information than it can digest. In any congressional office reams of
documents arrive every day and most are thrown in the round
file. Only to a limited extent does Congress digest information
and decide issues on a rational basis. It is primarily a political
arena, a place where issues are debated in a political, not
academic or rational context.

Focusing on procedure tells us a good deal about what
Congress will not do; we must also look at what it can and will
do. As I see it, Congress performs three basic roles fairly well.

The first and most obvious is as a conduit for constituent
views. It is, in fact, the only federal institution where the
people's wishes are fed directly into the system. For example, it
is an important sounding board, revealing how effectively
federal programs function or how a proposed course of action
will be received. As a sounding board it is not perfect; special
interests are overrepresented, and its votes do not always
indicate the general will. Still, what is debated on the floor of

Congress is important, and the mood of Congress, reflected in these debates, is rarely very far from the mood of the country at large.

The second role of Congress is general overseer of government policies and resource allocation. In this role its actions are not unlike those of a board of trustees. With very few exceptions Congress is not where policy is initiated. Most congressional committees or subcommittees have no overall plan or policy to attempt to implement in their area of concern. The Compensation Subcommittee of the House Armed Services Committee, for example, has no guiding policy about the structure of pay and allowances in the armed forces. The subcommittee rarely initiates legislation; it reviews, questions, and periodically modifies what the executive proposes. In performing this role, subcommittee members enjoy certain advantages. Often they have years of experience and know what has been tried before. They have communication lines to branches of the armed forces that provide them with information the executive may not have; and they are more sensitive than a Pentagon manager to conflicting pressures that build up around any policy change.

Congress's third role is to act as guardian of the processes of government—i. e., to establish and protect procedure. In many ways this is the most intriguing of the three roles. By establishing new procedures, which are, of course, ostensibly neutral, Congress often is able to effect substantive changes.

A good example is the National Environmental Protection Act (NEPA). Congress required that for any major federal project which would significantly affect the quality of the environment an environmental impact statement had to be written by the agency undertaking the project. This provision would force federal agencies to consider the environmental impact of a project before it was carried out. What happened, of course, was much more fundamental. Environmental groups around the country found they could use NEPA to bring suit against any federal agency that did not comply fully with its procedures. Once an environmental impact statement is written, environmentalists can use the statement as a source of objections to the proposed project. The impact statement forced federal agencies into discussions with environmentalists, and where the environmentalists were able to make a convincing case, it became politically difficult to ignore them.

As a result, NEPA brought a new group, environmentalists, into a decision-making process from which they previously had been excluded. A long series of projects regarded as dangerous to the environment—from nuclear reactors to public works (one of the most famous being the Cross-Florida Barge Canal)—were halted. By establishing this new procedure, Congress wrought changes more significant than any it might have voted in dealing with each project individually.

New procedures established by Congress produce substantive change by changing the decision-making process or bringing new people into it. Sometimes the direct impact of such legislation proves less important than the indirect results. For example, Congress in 1961 passed the Symington Amendment, which required that in allocating foreign economic aid, consideration be given to the resources that a recipient country assigns to defense. If a country's defense spending were excessive, the president should withhold aid. The direct impact of that amendment was nil; no country's aid was withdrawn for spending too much on the military. But the indirect impact was considerable. A committee chaired by the Agency for International Development (AID) now had to be included in policy decisions that until then had been managed solely by the Pentagon. It was included because should Congress wish to investigate compliance with this amendment, AID would then be asked if they had been consulted. As an indirect result of the Symington Amendment, a new group of people with a wholly different outlook was brought into the decision-making process.

Historically, Congress has used a vast number of procedural devices to alter the decision-making process. Structural change is one. Congress has established organizations and abolished them; it has increased their influence by having them report directly to the president, or decreased it by having them report to a third-ranking official. If Congress does not think that arms control is being given sufficient consideration by the executive branch, it can create an agency with independent access to the

White House, as it did with the Arms Control and Disarmament Agency (ACDA).

A second procedural device is to require certain findings before specific programs may be carried out. The Walsh Act of 1935 required that before the administration could transfer destroyers to another country, the Navy first had to certify they were not needed. Senator David I. Walsh, the author of the act, feared that President Roosevelt was about to give destroyers to Britain and thus drag the United States into another European war. While the senator's purpose was to prevent President Roosevelt from giving destroyers to Britain, he assumed Congress would be reluctant to give that order directly. He thus decided on a procedural device that would be acceptable to Congress. As Senator Walsh no doubt anticipated, the Navy was not willing to declare it had too many destroyers.

A third procedural device is for Congress to designate a specific official to make certain decisions. Placing responsibility for a decision in an office with predictable political or organizational interests naturally influences the decision. The act that established the Naval Petroleum Reserve, for example, requires that any decision to release petroleum from the reserves must be approved by the secretary of the Navy. Any Navy secretary will be reluctant to make such a determination.

Finally, Congress can involve already existing groups in government decisions by making them part of a new procedure. This might be a citizen group (such as the environmentalists in the NEPA case), it might be an agency of government, or perhaps even Congress itself. Sometimes the people brought into a decision do not belong to an identifiable group. For instance, under the provisions of the War Powers Act, if the president commits American forces to hostilities abroad, he must report to Congress within forty-eight hours his reasons for doing so, and at the end of sixty days he must withdraw those forces unless Congress votes to continue the commitment. By establishing this procedure, Congress had made itself the final arbiter on whether troops should be used. But, as we have seen, Congress is never happy in such a role and is most unlikely to challenge a president in such a foreign-policy decision. Indeed, liberals objected that the War Powers Act was too weak: bringing Congress into the decision would not change anything because Congress would simply rubber-stamp whatever the president had already decided to do.

But the liberal objection overlooks the effect of this bill on decision making in the executive branch. When the president considers sending troops somewhere, he and his advisers now know that the decision will provoke an intense debate for up to sixty days. Congressional committees will hold hearings, newspapers will write editorials, "Meet the Press" and "Face the Nation" will cross-examine government spokesmen; there will be network specials, demonstrations, and letters from constituents. The predictability of all this commotion is bound to strengthen the hand of those in the president's council who oppose military intervention. They can now object not with their own arguments but with the kind the president will inevitably have to face. Congress's ultimate verdict is not the most important factor; what is important is that the president and his advisers know their policy will receive intense public scrutiny. They will be much less inclined to embark upon a military adventure without a very strong case for it.

The ways in which Congress has used procedure in the past suggest that procedural changes offer the best hope of attacking many of today's problems, including arms control and weapons procurement.

One of the major problems in controlling procurement of new weapons is the "requirements" syndrome, under which every weapon requested by the military services is quickly defined as essential to fulfilling their military mission. Weapons systems become "requirements" very early in the process—well before Congress ever sees them as specific budget items. By the time Congress comes face to face with a new weapon, service and bureaucratic momentum is already behind it, contractors and unions are interested, and it is probably too late to stop it. What is needed is a vehicle for bringing other decision makers into the process sooner, perhaps a procedure requiring the president to act on major weapons in the early stages of development. Legislation could also mandate that advice be submitted to the president from experts who do not have a parochial interest in a follow-on system for every weapon in the inventory.

One procedure for dealing with the weapons-requirement syndrome might be the following: the president is required by Congress to give his approval before any research and development money is spent, and any weapons system to cost more than x billion dollars. Before making his decision, the president receives the independent views of the secretary of defense, the secretary of state, each of the service chiefs, the head of ACDA, and the president's science advisor. Each would be required to: (1) estimate the long-term cost of the weapons system; (2) estimate costs of alternative ways of accomplishing the same mission; and (3) evaluate the new system's impact on future arms control agreements. If this procedure, or something like it, were established, some of the most expensive and most destabilizing weapons proposed might be stopped before they gathered irresistible bureaucratic momentum.

Of course, new procedures do not guarantee correct decisions. All one can seek to guarantee is that more critical minds will have some influence before crucial decisions are made. It is also possible that the executive branch will subvert a procedure once it is established, although doing so would have its political risks and costs. Influencing decision making through procedural change may seem to be influencing it at the margin; certainly it operates one degree removed from the actual issues. But since Congress works that way, when it works at all, it seems to me the best hope for affecting the substance of decisions.

Congress is essentially a political institution and responds primarily to political stimuli. Rational arguments in such an institution carry little weight unless they are supported by political organization. Political organization can be mobilized around a national issue, but only with a great deal of effort. Usually, congressmen deal substantively and directly only with issues that are noncontroversial or with which they feel comfortable—those within their expertise or with which they have dealt previously. If an issue is controversial and unfamiliar, as most important issues are, Congress will instinctively begin groping toward a procedural resolution.

Congress as an institution is conservative, cautious and

reluctant to initiate change. It responds to old stimuli more quickly than to new ones. When it opposes the executive, it is usually to protect some interest group or some aspect of the status quo. New initiatives on the federal scene rarely are a product of Congress. An individual member or a group of members may take the initiative; but Congress as an institution rarely does.

In earlier days when the executive was smaller and the issues Congress dealt with were fewer and less intricate, there was more balance between the two branches. That balance exists no more. The executive has grown and its agencies have become highly specialized. Congress must deal with all the issues. It has remained (except for some increase in staff) roughly the same size, even though the number of yea and nay votes House members confronted rose from 159 in 1947-48 to 810 in 1975-76. Apart from the workload, Congress is much the same as Congress was; the executive is not as the executive was.

On arms control, as on many other subjects, the direct role that Congress can be expected to play is limited. In the jockeying that goes on within the government over our defense policies, the actions Congress can take will be either too broad or too narrow to be very constructive—either lopping 5 percent off the top of the entire defense budget or cutting the number of enlisted men working as servants for generals. The defense committees in Congress could be more effective, but because of their composition and outlook they will not be. Nor will Congress play a direct role in such traditional areas of arms control as negotiating with the Russians. SALT is too complicated, too much a field for experts.

Congress, however, cannot be ignored. Even if the SALT treaties did not have to be ratified by the Senate, the mood of Congress, reflecting the mood of the country, would define the limits within which an acceptable treaty must fall. But Congress's ideas about future arms control initiatives will be limited to such conceptually simple items as a comprehensive test ban, and even then only a minority will delve into the subject.

The failure of Congress to assume leadership in this and other areas is one reason for the great interest, and limited progress, in congressional reform. But reform, while a worthy goal in itself, is not likely to result in congressional leadership. The problem with Congress is its members: how they regard their job and how they make their decisions. It is possible, of course, that in time new people elected to Congress will bring with them new attitudes, and Congress will reassert itself. But that should not be counted on; the new members will find themselves in the same position as the old. They, too, will want to be reelected. They, too, will be subjected to conflicting pressures, will feel a lack of expertise, and will have little time to devote to any single issue.

Rather than try to make Congress into something it is not (that is, an alternative to the executive branch as an initiator of new ideas), we should look realistically at what Congress is and see if there are ways to improve its performance. Congress is a channel for constituent concerns; this role could be improved by lessening the influence of special interests. Congress is a board of trustees over government programs and policies; this function also, could be strengthened by an increasing emphasis on oversight and investigation. Congress guards the procedures of government; and while it prefers procedure over policy, it could do better in this area if it consciously chose to *use* procedures rather than to hide behind them to avoid directly confronting an issue.

This may seem a pessimistic assessment of Congress's capacities, and perhaps it is. But, as the NEPA case demonstrates, manipulation of procedure can be a very powerful weapon. Right now it is a weapon that is understood instinctively by some members of Congress and not at all by many.

Those who want to change U.S. arms control policy through Congress must consider not only what they want to do but also how it can be done. One way is to organize sufficient political muscle to effect the change. But issues on which this can be done are relatively rare. The other way is to devise some means of accomplishing the change procedurally. Congress feels more comfortable dealing with issues this way. More important, using procedure makes it possible to gain enough votes to win.

4
Politics of the Purse
Thomas A. Dine

Introduction

In the nuclear age the original Constitutional responsibilities of the legislative and executive branches have been reversed. The Founding Fathers intended Congress to propose national policy and enact new programs, and the president, armed with a veto, to be the agent of restraint. Today, the president initiates most major legislation, while Congress is left to modify or defeat executive proposals. In granting Congress control over the nation's money, the Constitution also gave Congress control over the nation's defense. The "military policy of the United States is shaped by the Congress, not by the armed forces," General Omar Bradley recognized over a quarter of a century ago, because "Congress controls the appropriations which, in the final analysis, control military policy."[1] The ultimate use of such leverage was made on June 29, 1973, when Congress passed provisos ending United States engagement in hostilities anywhere in Indochina by August 15

The views expressed here are entirely those of the author. The Senate Budget Committee, where the author is director of the National Security Group, bears no responsibility for the contents or the opinions.

of that year. Since World War II, however, Congress has rarely exercised its power to impose defense policy on the president.

Even though annual defense outlays currently exceed a quarter of all federal expenditures each year—now more than $100 billion a year and expected to reach $150 billion by the mid 1980s—disputes over military budgets on Capitol Hill seldom transcend the mundane. Debate has focused on such subjects as financial adjustments, military real estate, constituent contract and personnel services, the Reserves and National Guard, the political activities of certain generals, and insignificant aspects of weapons decisions already made.[2] Congress has had little voice in determining overall spending levels for the country's defense budget, and has seemed content to follow the lead of the president and the Joint Chiefs of Staff. In debate over the defense budget for Fiscal Year 1977, Congress specifically left the future of the B-1 strategic bomber to the president. Jimmy Carter responded on June 30, 1977, announcing his decision not to proceed with production, but to emphasize instead development of the cruise missile. Only two days earlier, the House of Representatives, not wanting to confront the Democratic president, had rejected by a 65-vote margin an amendment deleting $1.43 billion for B-1 production from the Fiscal 1978 Defense Appropriations bill. Following the president's televised news conference, the Senate, by an almost two-to-one vote, concurred with his decision. As Senator Barry Goldwater admitted, although he opposed Carter's decision, "I cannot see any sense in appropriating money for a weapon system that the President has declared he does not want."[3]

Defense decisions on Capitol Hill have concentrated on pork barrel advantages rather than policy outcomes or program results. Budget priorities, long-range planning, analysis of the relative value of strategic and general purpose forces, weapons trade-offs, and cost-benefit analyses—all these have, until the last few years, been avoided.[4] In brief, Congress has consistently and frequently declined what Edwin S. Corwin described as the Constitutional "invitation to struggle for the privilege of directing" national defense policy.[5]

To strengthen its capacity to control the budget—and thus policy—and to confront presidential dominance by asserting its own priorities and prerogatives in the federal budget process, the legislative branch in 1974 passed the Congressional Budget and Impoundment Control Act (the Budget Act).[6] There were several motives: growing distress over the troubled state of the economy; disillusionment with the Kennedy-Johnson-Nixon guns and butter policies; concern about the loss of control over future federal spending and the annual deficit; and a realization that unchecked defense and budget policies had led the country into Vietnam. The new congressional budget process attempts to redress the imbalance between the legislative and executive branches and return to the division of powers and responsibilities envisioned by the Founding Fathers.

Advocates of arms control, interested in paring the military budget and eliminating certain strategic systems altogether, have supported the new budget system. They recognize that the process will not by itself tame the spiraling arms race, but hope that it might provide the long-sought handle to reduce the level of military spending. "It may be possible," Congressman Les Aspin, a former Defense Department official but now that department's most persistent critic, wrote in early 1975, "by shifting power from the defense committees to the . . . Budget Committee, to change the way Congress handles defense budgets."[7] Disarmament lobbies like the Arms Control Association and SANE predicted that the new process would make it possible to place a ceiling on arms expenditures. "The new budget procedures have provided the means for a more careful scrutiny of military spending in relation to the budget as a whole than has been possible before," concluded an article in a SANE newsletter.[8]

In this essay the effects the new budget procedure has had on defense spending will be explored. Has the process altered the way Congress looks at military requests? Has it provided Congress with a base of useful information and alternative policies? What effect has it had on arms control? Does more rational analysis and thus management of defense costs really have the potential of "saving the world?"[9]

The Process and Defense Spending

Historically, Congress's institutional reforms have tended to buttress the independent exercise of legislative power. An

example is the broadening of the Armed Services Committees'
authority over weapons acquisition. To gain a grip on the
growing military budget, the committees have required that
innovations or major alterations in the procurement of aircraft,
missiles, naval vessels, and certain land warfare vehicles, as
well as research and development, be passed on by Congress
twice each year: new weapons systems must first be voted
authorization, then, in a separate measure, appropriations.[10]
This increased the importance of the authorizing process,
giving the committees more control over arms.[11]

The reforms mandated in the Budget Act go beyond
any previous efforts to strengthen legislative policymaking.
In fact, they are widely considered the most important
change in the budget process since the 1921 Budget and
Accounting Act. Congress now has a way to establish and
examine the aggregate as well as the functional budget; it has a
comprehensive method of setting budget priorities.[12]

The congressional budget timetable requires enactment of
two concurrent resolutions (which do not require the
president's signature) on the budget before the beginning of
each fiscal year, October 1. The First Concurrent Resolution,
with its aggregate and functional spending and revenue
targets, must be adopted by May 15; the Second Concurrent
Resolution, with its aggregate and functional spending
ceilings and revenue floor, by September 15.

Setting defense spending levels is inextricably linked to the
work requirements implicit in this timetable. A significant
portion of military funds are potentially subject to close
scrutiny; the same is true of the planning, programming, and
budgeting activities of the Defense Department. Approxi-
mately 65 percent of the department's budget is controllable
and subject to annual review (75 percent of the federal budget is
considered relatively uncontrollable, being dictated for the
most part by previously enacted entitlement programs). Less
money for defense during the Vietnam War meant diminished
American participation in the conflict and, eventually,
withdrawal. Less money for defense now potentially means
more for education, health, and social welfare. Or, as the debate
over the First Concurrent Resolution for Fiscal 1978 demon-

strated, defense and domestic demands can now receive equal emphasis.

Before examining the interaction between the new congressional budget process and defense spending over the past three years, it would be useful to look first at the reasons advanced to explain congressional reluctance to question military expenditures.

Executive Expertise

The most common explanation for congressional acquiescence in the Defense Department's proposals is that senators and congressmen feel ill-equipped to judge defense programs. The impact of the isolationists' antimilitary activities of the late 1930s, the military's successful prosecution of World War II, and the emergency environment of the Cold War have all led legislators to eschew deep involvement in national security affairs. The assumption has been that military judgments are best left to military professionals. J. Ronald Fox, former assistant secretary of the Army, reports a conversation he had with a congressional staff member that highlights this attitude. "A general comes over here [to Congress] and they pat him on the shoulder and say, 'How are things going, General?' If the general says 'O.K.,' then they are relaxed." Commenting on the highly controversial C-5A transport aircraft program, Senator Margaret Chase Smith—at the time, ranking Republican on the Senate Armed Services Committee—said, "Of course, I can only take the word of those who know more about it than I do."[13]

A variation on this dependency theme is the generally accepted notion that the American voter supports programs to maintain national strength in a hostile world, and that politically it makes sense to defer to those who manage such programs. Senator Richard Russell, chairman of the Senate Armed Services Committee, warned in the late 1950s, "God help the American people if Congress starts legislating military strategy."[14]

The leaders of the Armed Services and Appropriations Committees in both houses have consistently supported programs the military labeled vital to national security, particularly those involving nuclear weapons. Russell and like-minded legislators, always suspicious of Soviet motives and thus maximalist defense spenders, believed—and still believe—that the United States should maintain nuclear superiority.[15] Consequently, strategic systems in general and the Triad (land-based missiles, submarines, manned bombers) in particular, have, until the last few years, been questioned least. The national interest vis-à-vis the Soviet Union is best defined, according to adherents of this view, by generals and admirals and their civilian allies in the Defense Department.

The Information Gap

In formulating national security policy Congress is hampered by a serious information gap. Control of information means control of policymaking. The executive branch, with a foreign policy-defense-intelligence community of four and a half million people, has monopolized the collection, analysis, and control of data. Most members of Congress have removed themselves from the information-gathering process, relying on information supplied by the executive or by newspapers.

The executive has manipulated access to information to keep Capitol Hill at bay. Congress has dealt reasonably well with structural issues such as management and pay; the information, often supplied by special interest groups, is public. Congress has not effectively participated in larger defense budget decisions, however, being excluded from the debate and consensus building within the Defense Department. In *The Common Defense* Samuel Huntington described how coherent choices between competing strategic programs are developed in the planning dialogue conducted by the Joint Chiefs of Staff, Defense Department civilians, and from time to time, the National Security Council. Positions, constituencies, and leverage diverge as they do within Congress. What finally emerges from the executive branch is supported by a coalition strong enough to carry the day in Congress.

For long-range purposes the first annual budget request for an individual defense program is often deliberately understated by the Defense Department; the object is to obtain initial congressional authorization. Once this foot is in the door, full funding is inevitable. "If we told the truth to the Congress," a Pentagon program manager admitted, "we would never get our programs approved. So we have to understate the cost and overstate the performance."[16] The experience of Senator Thomas J. McIntyre, chairman of the Armed Services Subcommittee on Research and Development, is illustrative: "We had been unable either to eliminate or substantially affect a single program getting ready to emerge from the far end of the pipeline," he recounted. "I have discovered, much to my own frustration, that the present viewpoint seems to be that we are committed to a system's ultimate production as soon as we have sunk virtually any money into it. This is an attitude we will have to change. There is no way, even with the savings which an end to our involvement in Vietnam will produce, that we could avoid a substantial increase in the total defense budget if we went into production on all the major systems now in the [research and development] pipeline."[17]

Secrecy within the legislative branch perpetuates this information gap. With most meetings, hearings, mark-up sessions, and conferences held behind closed doors "in the interest of national security," members' attendance and attentiveness, their preparation and comprehension, the skill and skepticism of their questioning, have been hidden from public observation. For too long, probing by the two authorizing committees and the two appropriations subcommittees has been desultory. Despite a "lengthy exposure to Congressional committees, Pentagon witnesses are seldom questioned in depth," Fox reported. "The 'hard' questions— questions which might help Congress to determine which new and ongoing defense programs are essential to national defense, which programs are redundant or nonessential, and which programs should be reconstructed, cut back, or cancelled because of poor management or faulty performance—are rarely asked."[18] Only in recent years have a few hearings been open; nongovernment witnesses are now allowed to testify, but not extensively or alongside executive branch officials.

Members have resisted enriching their own knowledge and that of the relevant committees. Until the formation of the Senate and House Budget Committees and the congressional Budget Office, there were fewer than fifty professional staff members in Congress assigned to scrutinizing the defense budget. Of the fifteen standing committees in the Senate in 1977, the Committee on Armed Services was fourteenth in professional staff size; the House Armed Services Committee ranked thirteenth out of twenty. The Senate Foreign Relations Committee assigned one person to staff strategic arms control issues. With barely more than two dozen staff members each, these crucial committees clearly have insufficient analytic resources to oversee military legislation. Yet the Defense Department in Fiscal 1977 assigned 333 people to handle congressional relations, at a salary cost of $7,400,000. The department also had another 1,322 employees working on public affairs, at a salary cost of $20,721,000.[19]

The longstanding unwillingness of Congress to act as a separate branch, to establish and then to rely on its own information base, reflects structural deficiencies in the institution itself. Although working at a disadvantage— without back-up support, without computers, without member concern—the congressional staff has recently played a fundamental part in decisions on defense spending, and will play an even more crucial role in the years ahead.[20]

Electoral Politics

The Roosevelt maxim "You have to get elected before you can do anything" is basic to understanding legislative behavior. According to the research of David Mayhew, members are "single-minded seekers of reelection." Politics is the most important determinant of congressional behavior. It explains Congress's consistent disengagement from conflict with the executive over questionable defense spending. Votes on military issues display a calculus that varies from state to state and district to district; votes do not reflect a coherent congressional consensus on defense. They do reflect the strong desire of most congressmen to take public positions that will not cost them votes in the next election.[21]

In the nuclear age, given strong concerns throughout the country with the Soviet Union's foreign policy and military strength, members tend to support the military establishment. It is generally believed that there is nothing to gain and much to lose with voters and with fellow members in criticizing the Defense Department or countering the president. To vote against military appropriations is to risk being labeled disloyal, soft on communism, or encouraging another Pearl Harbor. Although a decade of opposition to American intervention in Indochina and revelations of Pentagon mismanagement have altered this sentiment somewhat, external events such as Moscow's ventures in the Middle East and Africa and its military modernization efforts—including what is at least perceived to be nuclear parity with the United States—have maintained a climate of opinion favoring high American defense spending.

Most members of Congress can see little political gain in the hard work and complicated analyses necessary to conduct a proper review of Defense Department proposals and then possibly to offer alternatives. "It is a misallocation of resources" by members "to devote time and energy to prescription or scrutiny . . . unless credit is available for legislative maneuvering," Mayhew concluded. "On matters where credit-claiming possibilities wear thin, therefore, we should not be surprised to find that members display only a modest interest in what . . . passage accomplishes."[22]

Members are also inhibited by a concern for their position among their peers. Crusaders such as Senator William Proxmire or Congressman Aspin do receive political credit in Wisconsin and in arms control circles for critical evaluation of the military budget. But in return for their probing and regular press releases, the two are regarded as "outsiders" by their colleagues. Congressional decision making, concluded Craig Liske and Barry Runquist after studying the Cheyenne helicopter and MBT-70 tank cases, "seems dominated by concern for maintaining or advancing the decision-maker's political position within the Congress or some other salient political area."[23]

Instead of confronting defense issues directly, members handle complicated budget accounts and technology indirectly, by shifting the focus from substance to procedure. The policy merits or cost-benefit demerits of a potential purchase are avoided; as Aspin puts it elsewhere in this volume, members are "most comfortable dealing with national security matters in procedural terms; there they are the experts."

When a major change in military policy involves political costs, actual or possible, an elected policymaker generally resorts to the first rule of politics: don't stick your neck out.

Internal Procedures

Decisions are made in Congress as a result of members' bargaining and compromising with one another; with the electoral connection so strong, members seek to maximize individual and group interests. Subjective preferences prevail over objective reasoning, which places Congress at a disadvantage in analyzing defense strategies in depth.

Aaron Wildavsky observed in the 1960s that Congress's fragmented approach to funding decisions precluded a comprehensive review of any agency's programs. He argued that Congress acts sensibly when it forces changes at the margin. Further, line item budgeting makes consensus easier to achieve. Program or mission budgeting focuses debate on comprehensive or controversial issues which are difficult to resolve by political bargaining.[24]

Yet a major negative consequence of incremental budgeting has been preoccupation with current expenditures. In the defense budget a favorite Appropriations Committee target is the operation and maintenance account; a cut results in no money being spent. Similarly, in procurement the decision to delay purchasing a ship reduces spending in the fiscal year under review. But when it comes to the very costly military compensation and retirement system, a cut has only limited current impact. The effect of a reform, though in the long run substantial, would not be felt for several years after enactment.

How has the new budget process fared against these obstacles?

Fiscal Year 1976: The Power of the Purse

The new congressional budget process made its debut in January 1975, with the convening of the 94th Congress. Owing to the worst recession since 1958, both houses decided to commence work on the Fiscal 1976 budget immediately in accordance with the new procedures, rather than waiting for Fiscal 1977, as the Budget Act had envisioned. By the end of the session the institution of congressional budget control was in place, and the economy began making a recovery. Defense spending became the centerpiece of debate over the Fiscal 1976 budget, as it was again for Fiscal 1978. Members relied heavily on the new budget procedures to argue for lower spending levels.

Contrasting themes were established early. The Ford administration requested $107.7 billion in budget authority and $94 billion in outlays for national defense functions. Secretary of Defense James Schlesinger asserted that reductions in these record-high amounts would place the United States second to the Soviet Union in military power. The combination of inflation, pay increases, and legislative spending cuts, he said, were "chopping away" at the military budget so that in terms of real purchasing power, defense spending had dropped below pre–Vietnam War levels. Fiscal 1976 was the year to reverse this trend, or the Soviet Union would achieve a "preponderance" of military strength by about 1978. "If the Defense Department budget is to be reduced," Schlesinger warned, "it should be done in clear recognition that we will not be able to fulfill our responsibilities."[25]

Less predictably, Schlesinger challenged Congress to debate openly the assumptions, processes, and weapons systems that make up U.S. policy. By chance, this challenge came just as the new Budget Committees were beginning to apply new approaches—competition between programs and systems analysis—in analyzing the defense budget.

Senator Alan Cranston, a member of the Senate Budget Committee and the most outspoken of those interested in reordering the nation's spending priorities, responded to the challenge. "I am hopeful . . . we will find ways to provide more money for such programs as education, if more can be demonstrated to be needed," he told the National School Board Association Legislative Conference, "while spending less in certain places where I *know* less is in order; such as, less for our over-bloated . . . wasteful defense budget . . . the biggest peacetime budget for military matters for any nation in the history of the world." Moreover, "we must cut back on the $5 billion we presently spend annually on military aid to 57 dictators."[26]

Senator Lawton Chiles, also a Budget Committee member, wrote the chairman, Edmund S. Muskie, to request that the "Budget Committee provide, for the first time, a forum for examining higher-order decisions of defense policy and strategy which can be clearly linked to budget actions."[27] Both Chiles and Muskie, joined later by Senator Henry Bellmon, the committee's ranking Republican, urged the Defense Department to furnish a mission area budget, so that Congress could analyze defense spending in terms of the total resources devoted to major military missions and evaluate them in the context of foreign policy and defense strategies. The Defense Department, in concert with the committee, complied in Fiscal 1979.

The two Budget Committees took different approaches in their Fiscal 1976 reviews. The House Budget Committee, proceeding from the president's original request and views and estimates from the Appropriations Subcommittee on Defense and the Armed Services Committee, focused on such specific issues as what inflation rate should be used in allocating funds for Defense Department purchases, and what effect the continuing increase in unobligated and unexpended balances in the defense budget would have on the Fiscal 1976 request.[28]

The Senate Budget Committee, under pressure to keep the national deficit to a minimum, looked for areas of management savings. It also considered overall policy, trying to relate foreign policy, national security, force level, manpower, and budgetary considerations. In the effort to link defense strategy and spending, these questions were raised:

1. How much money should be allocated to the strategic force structure given the Vladivostok accords and the possible success of SALT II?
2. How large should the general purpose forces be, and what proportion of them deployed overseas? How much modernization do they need?[29]

Tensions between the Senate Budget Committee and the

Pentagon surfaced during the committee's mark-up of the First Concurrent Resolution, setting overall expenditure targets for Fiscal 1976. The committee initially voted to cut $3.6 billion in outlays from the requested $94 billion. This approach was abandoned twenty-four hours later, after a few members were persuaded by Defense Department spokesmen that such a cut was too deep and would leave as many as 175,000 persons jobless in a recessionary economy. Cranston called the argument "hypothetical" and "misleading,"[30] but the committee restored $800 million to the outlay target. This struggle between maximalist and minimalist defense spenders was the opening salvo in a contest that continued throughout the legislative session.

In introducing the Budget Committee's version of the First Concurrent Resolution in April 1975, Muskie told his Senate colleagues: "The Budget and Impoundment Control Act of 1974 is not a bookkeeping tool. It is a policy instrument that gives us new control over the direction America takes."[31] Muskie gave these words substance in midsummer. The conference report on the Military Procurement Authorization bill became a major test of the new budget process. As reported from the Armed Services Committees' conference on July 25, the bill threatened the budget targets Congress had adopted in May. Although it was an authorization measure and did not directly provide funds, the one-third of the national defense budget it covered was large enough to set the pattern for appropriations bills that would follow. Historically, the difference between authorization and appropriation levels for military spending is marginal. If the conference report had been adopted and the totals it authorized fully appropriated, it would have demolished the budget targets recommended by the Budget Committees in the First Concurrent Resolution.

Muskie decided to make an all-out effort to enforce the budget targets. In doing so, he joined other defense minimalists on the committee—Cranston, Joe Biden, Jim Abourezk, and Walter Mondale—who were already committed to voting against the report. The chairman sent a letter to all Senate Budget Committee members on July 28, seeking their support. Two days later, he unleashed his most potent weapon— bipartisan support. Muskie and Bellmon sent a letter to every senator, telling of the signers' intention to oppose both the Military Procurement Authorization and Child Nutrition Act (school lunch) Amendments conference reports. "We cannot hold the federal deficit under the $68.8 billion level specified in the [congressional] budget if we ignore authorization and entitlement programs which clearly imply spending in excess of the budget target," they wrote.[32] The bipartisan message gave both moderate Democrats and conservative Republicans on the committee assurance that they could join the coalition without being hurt politically back home. Muskie carried the argument to the Senate floor. "If Congress decides to breach a spending target," he said, "it is actually making a judgment to increase the deficit. . . . But there is another factor. The Budget Reform Act has two purposes—to control federal spending and cut waste, and to reorder our national priorities within an overall spending ceiling. These two conference reports provide both guns and butter—more in each case than Congress has targeted. Both should be rejected."[33] A budget control coalition had formed; the offensive was in full gear.

In challenging the Pentagon and the two Committees on Armed Services, procedure became all-important. As noted earlier, this is an area in which members feel at home. The sanctity of procedure was invoked; its invocation served to gain members the time they needed to collect information and analyze, a goal that had only recently come to be regarded as at all feasible. For example, the Armed Services Committees' conference report included an authorization of $60 million for a long-lead-time procurement of the nuclear strike cruiser. The administration had submitted a budget amendment inserting this new item six days before the fiscal year began; it was added in conference at the urging of Admiral Hyman Rickover and Congressman Charles Bennett of the House Armed Services Committee. Senators found this maneuver totally inconsistent with the intent of the Budget Act, especially in view of the cruiser's major long-range budget implications. Acceptance would have committed Congress to approving a $1.2 billion ship in Fiscal 1977. The vessel was the opening wedge in a shipbuilding program with projected costs of $30 billion. "Accepting the $60 million item," Muskie wrote his committee colleagues, "contravenes the basic aim of the Act . . . and poses a dangerous precedent for the future."[34] In response, and on the defensive for one of the few times in his career, Senator John Stennis, Russell's successor as chairman of the Armed Services Committee, claimed, "The procurement of the ship itself will be a matter for future Congressional action."[35]

Also invoking procedural arguments, but on the other side, Senate Appropriations Committee Chairman John L. McClellan claimed the whole debate was over "a very small issue" and the work of the Senate Armed Services Committee did not warrant "a repudiation." "It would be such a burden—if not torture—to send these conferees back and have them go through this long ordeal again," he said, "when everything is in, this bill, if it does exceed the budget, will have a review. It still has to be appropriated, and everything in the appropriation bill that exceeds what the Budget Committee thinks is proper is subject to amendment, subject to change, subject to debate, and the issue can be resolved."[36] Senator Robert Taft, a conferee, urged reverting to another standard Capitol Hill procedure, with the two houses splitting the difference in conference. He asked Muskie if it weren't institutional tradition to compromise. Muskie replied, "When you have got a budget target that is binding on both Houses, tradition has to give way to a greater extent to the imperatives of the question of budget."[37]

Bellmon, holding firm on the principle of fiscal restraint, adamantly opposed the school lunch conference report as well, because it would have meant spending almost $430 million over the target. Also, it was entitlement legislation and thus an automatic spending measure. "This plunge into economic chaos has to be stopped," he said. "I consider it to be the greatest threat our country faces today. . . . I am absolutely convinced that this country must be just as strong economically as it must be prepared militarily. . . . Military need must be weighed carefully with other needs and the ability of this nation to meet the cost of Government."[38]

Because the debate had broadened beyond simple name-calling to issues of budget analysis and fiscal restraint plus congressional procedure, the Senate rejected the conference report on military procurement, 48 to 42. Senator George McGovern immediately postponed Senate consideration of his $2.9 billion conference report on the Child Nutrition Act. Thus was won the first major test of fiscal and budget control.

The second conference was concluded on September 17. The conferees removed $250 million from the military procurement bill, including the $60 million lead funds for the nuclear strike cruiser.

The fledgling process, passing on to the appropriations phase, put enormous pressure on the chairmen of the Appropriations Committees, George Mahon and McClellan.[39] On September 25 the House Appropriations Committee, to stay within the budget target, cut $7.6 billion from the president's request. Shortly thereafter, Secretary Schlesinger branded the House cuts "deep, savage, and arbitrary."[40] In response, Chairman Mahon said, "I believe that most Americans would agree that $90.2 billion for the Defense Department is, if managed and spent wisely, adequate at a time when no United States military forces are engaged in combat and the Nation is faced with a huge deficit and an increase in the national debt of $80 billion this year."[41] That the department asked for restoration of only $2.6 billion out of the $7.6 billion cut indicates "there was some cushion put in the original request," he argued.[42]

In early October McClellan sent a letter to Muskie requesting "a formal indication of how H.R. 9861 [the Defense Appropriations bill] as passed by the House compares with that contemplated in the First Concurrent Resolution, so our Members will know in advance of [Senate] subcommittee action where the House bill stands." Muskie and Bellmon responded, "The First Concurrent Resolution Congress passed in May 1975 would be exceeded by $142 million in budget authority and $1,521 million in outlays."[43]

The Senate Appropriations Committee reported its version of the defense bill, paring $200 million less than the House. Because of subsequent conference action and the enactment of other bills at lower levels, the total appropriated for defense fell below the ceiling set in the Second Concurrent Resolution. The budget process itself put pressure on Congress to stay below the ceiling.[44] The discipline diminished pork-barreling. Members had to suggest equivalent cuts when proposing increases. It was no longer easy to agree to a colleague's suggested increase in exchange for a pet project of one's own. The new process forced individual members to legislate in terms of priorities. They could advert to the new budget process to justify value judgments, whereas previously there had been little political cost in trying to please everyone, but a good deal in trying to hold down spending.

Congress demonstrated in its Fiscal 1976 budget deliberations that it held some power over the military purse strings. This gave rise to a new spirit of aggressiveness: a new fund of information was at the disposal of Congress; just as important, a professional staff was at work on Congress's behalf, developing that information in ways most useful to members.

A bipartisan coalition supporting congressional control of all spending coalesced, particularly in the Senate Budget Committee. "We were in effect a couple of strangers," Bellmon has said of himself and Muskie, "but we decided that the process was so important to the country that it had to be made to work. I think both [Muskie] and I have been willing to submerge our personal preferences to the process and to speak in harmony. We have tried very hard to hold the whole committee together." Muskie said, "The most important thing this year is that the Senate and House have indicated a willingness to accept the discipline. I think it is do-able."[45]

Fiscal Year 1977: The Power of Politics

In its deliberations over fiscal 1977 Congress was officially operating in accordance with the Budget Act. The timetable was met; work on spending legislation was completed before the fiscal year began. All national security appropriations were voted on before October 1, 1976, for the first time since the Korean War. Moreover, in the aggregate the appropriations measures fell below the targets in the First Concurrent Resolution, which allowed the ceilings to be lowered in the Second Concurrent Resolution. Congress passed a Third Concurrent Resolution in March 1977 to include an economic stimulus package. Again, the defense ceilings were adjusted downward. The new budget process demonstrated its flexibility and staying power; its parameters were a fact of legislative life.

Members allowed outside influences to block sustained analysis of key military budget issues for Fiscal 1977. Congress recognized that decisions on these issues would have serious financial consequences for the following four years at least, but in a presidential election year the military budget became highly politicized. The mood in congress changed, and so did the congressional trend of cutting back on Pentagon requests. Chairman Mahon admitted that his House Appropriations Committee had decided early on this "was not the year to rock the boat."[46]

The Ford administration requested for national defense $114.9 billion (26.5 percent) of the total federal budget in a new budget authority, and $101.1 billion (25.6 percent) in outlays.[47] Only the Fiscal 1942 budget was proportionately larger.

The rationale for requesting this substantial increase in military funds was the upward trend of the Soviet Union's military budget. There was mounting evidence that the USSR was investing heavily in expanding and upgrading both strategic and conventional forces.[48] Majorities in both houses accepted the argument that American military spending had to increase, not only to offset inflation but to offset increases in Soviet strength. The next five budgets projected by the Defense Department were designed to overcome the Russians' lead. Drew Middleton, the *New York Times* military correspondent and an advocate of new weapons systems and long-range arms development, wrote that the United States "is taking too long to produce the weapons necessary for maintaining the present precarious equilibrium."[49]

A staff study, prepared for the Senate Budget Committee before its mark-up of the First Concurrent Resolution, looked into the security perceptions of the Soviet Union and the comparative force strengths of NATO and Warsaw Pact countries, as well as that of the two superpowers. The analysis showed that directly comparing the military expenditures of the two superpowers was not helpful. Spending trends, by contrast, were important.[50] Overall, the study concluded, "The USSR's armed forces have expanded in recent years to provide a 'visibly increased preponderance,' to use Foreign Minister

Gromyko's phrase, behind the country's foreign/military policy. . . . The forces in the field today are the result of decisions made before the Brezhnev policy of détente was enacted in 1972. The SALT-era decisions dealing with the deployment of new weapons are an unknown."[51]

Believing that the Soviet Union was proceeding with a rapid arms build-up and that prospects for a new SALT agreement were poor, the American people, said Mahon, were "in no mood to take a chance on the adequacy of defense." Because these same conditions would continue for several years, Mahon foresaw no possibility of reducing the defense budget to less than its current level.[52] At the committee mark-up, Senator Pete V. Domenici spoke for the majority when he said, "If I am going to err on this one, I am going to err on the long side because I am no longer convinced that the Soviet Union is building in response to anything we are doing but that the momentum is their own."[53]

Reinforcing this view was Moscow's support of anti-American factions in Angola and elsewhere in Africa. This aroused congressional concern about the Soviet Union's global intentions and undercut support for détente. Although an overwhelming majority voted to bar United States intervention in Angola, members felt that sharp reductions in the defense budget might be interpreted by friends and foes alike as evidence of isolationism. There was also apprehension on Capitol Hill over the direction the president and Secretary of State Henry Kissinger were taking in relations with the USSR. For instance, many members saw no benefit to the United States in our agreeing at Helsinki to the "inviolability" of all European borders. And why had Ford followed Kissinger's advice not to receive Alexander Solzhenitsyn at the White House? Nor was a satisfactory explanation given for Schlesinger's abrupt dismissal. Although he was not widely liked in Congress, Schlesinger was respected. After his firing, admiration for him broadened. When his succession by White House aide Donald Rumsfeld was announced, many members believed Ford had sacrificed competence for cronyism.

The Republican primary campaign led to a debate between President Ford and Ronald Reagan over the defense budget.

Reagan charged that the United States lagged behind the Soviet Union in military power, citing statistics sifted from Defense Department documents and congressional testimony by Pentagon officials. Rumsfeld, starting in January with the defense secretary's annual statement, repeatedly warned that if the spending trends were not reversed, the United States would fall behind the Soviet Union. Rumsfeld's warnings boomeranged against the president, making it awkward for administration officials to rebut Reagan's charges. The secretary of state, the defense secretary, chairman of the Joint Chiefs of Staff, and other spokesmen had to fall back on the reasoning of minimalist defense spenders.[54]

At a Budget Committee mark-up Senator Cranston charged that Ford and Reagan were "engaging in a stupid argument of 'Are we ahead of the Russians or are they ahead of us?' " The important questions, he said, are "What do we really need? What are we trying to protect?"[55] Senator Sam Nunn observed, "The capacity of election-year politics to simplify the most complex and difficult issue should never be underestimated." He added, "This year the knotty and intricate questions posed by what appears to be a significant shift in the military balance between the United States and the Soviet Union have been served up to the American public as a debate over whether the United States is the No. 1 or No. 2 military power in the world."[56] And Kissinger warned, "No service is done to the nation by those who portray an exaggerated specter of Soviet power and American weakness."[57] Reagan's campaign may have cost taxpayers an oversize defense budget, both initially and $1.2 billion more in supplemental requests for shipbuilding and other items related to the Texas primary.[58]

Election-year forces affected Democrats as well. Members who wanted to impose a lower ceiling on defense found themselves preoccupied with not becoming an easy target for their opponent. This was also true of the Democratic presidential nominee. As it turned out, while their Republican rivals attacked each other on the military preparedness issue, Jimmy Carter and Democratic senators and congressmen escaped unscathed. Later, Ford and Carter vied for the role of the sternest advocate of a "strong" national defense policy.

Perceptions of public opinion played a part, too. Military maximalists claimed Congress's shift to high defense spending in the Fiscal 1977 budget reflected "a change in U.S. public sentiment from a strong anti-military stance in the latter years of the Vietnam war to one that is unwilling to accept Russia's continuing drive for military superiority."[59] Hard data, however, did not corroborate this reading of public sentiment. A measured survey of public opinion on national security policy, conducted periodically since 1972 by Potomac Associates of Washington, D.C., concluded in May 1976 that the legacy of Vietnam still lingered. In foreign policy the American people "seek a coherent and positive approach that combines firmness and strength, reinforced allied relationships, wariness of a Soviet adversary that insists on playing the game of détente by its own rules, and a more carefully drawn definition of national security that would avoid an unwarranted intervention abroad leading to another Vietnam." In contrast to a decade or so earlier, international issues were no longer those of greatest public concern. "At the top of an enumeration of 31 problem areas were ten domestic issues. Only in eleventh place came keeping our military and defense forces strong."[60]

In completing the final resolution for Fiscal 1977, outgoing Chairman Brock Adams of the House Budget Committee summarized the first full cycle of the new budget procedure. "Perhaps the most important aspect of the final budget resolution of Fiscal Year 1977," he said, is that "it contains the budget of Congress and not that of the President." In alluding to defense, he noted the difficulty of the achievement. "In addition to our victories, we have suffered some defeats." But "the significance of this is that it demonstrates that Congress has now gained control of the budget. Without this control, we would have no hope of ever balancing the budget and getting a firm grip on Federal spending. You simply cannot achieve the one without the other."[61] The Fiscal 1977 budget marked an end to passive congressional acceptance of executive priorities.

The two Budget Committee staffs and the Congressional Budget Office examined allocations for particular programs in terms of how likely the outlays were to contribute to specific program objectives. Members voted dollars for the sixteen functional spending categories, including national defense, in terms of program goals, the evaluation of those goals, and competing claims of the different functional categories. In defense, as we have seen, politics played a large part in the evaluation. A majority of members decided to pay the high cost of military modernization and payrolls. Once this consensus was reached, however, the two Budget Committees closely monitored authorizing and appropriating committees' actions to ensure that budget authority and outlays in individual pieces of legislation met the overall target set in the three Budget Resolutions.

Fiscal Year 1978: Priorities of the Purse

In the third year of the new budget procedure, Congress took further steps toward assuring a coherent fiscal policy. Glimmerings of a focus on national needs also appeared in the Fiscal 1978 debate, particularly over the relative claims of defense and domestic spending.

The priorities debate first surfaced in the two executive branch budget requests. In his last budget President Ford called for curtailing social welfare expenditures but increasing those for national defense. Ford called for $123.1 billion in budget authority and $110.1 billion in outlays for the military, a 13 percent increase over the previous year's level. President Carter's adjustments to this proposal emphasized increased federal expenditures to stimulate recovery from the 1974-75 recession. In defense, fresh from his campaign pledge to reduce the budget by $5 to $7 billion, the new president initially made thirty-one specific changes, the net effect of which cut only $2.8 billion in budget authority and $300 million in outlays from the level recommended by Ford; a majority of the reductions were deferrals or stretchouts of existing weapons programs. After contentious considerations of budget levels, nuclear-powered aircraft carriers, the B-1 bomber, and the neutron bomb, the first session of the 95th Congress agreed to national defense ceilings of $116.4 billion in budget authority and $110.1 billion in outlays.

Overall, the Fiscal 1978 military budget—reshaped and

modified by Congress and a new administration—provided the third straight year of real program growth, with defense outlays absorbing about 24 percent of total federal outlays and 5.3 percent of the gross national product. This reflected a period of testing and testiness between the United States and the Soviet Union, as well as between Congress and the new president, and an economy still gripped by inflation, unemployment, and deficits.

The defense debate focused in part on the Soviet Union's gaining ground vis-à-vis the United States. The new defense secretary, Harold Brown, more cautious than his two predecessors, noted the build-up by the USSR in ground and tactical air forces and its ability to bring reinforcements in swiftly. Brown's response was to prepare both for short-warning attacks by the Warsaw Pact and the heavier attacks that could follow mobilization.[62] Persistent warnings about the Soviet Union ran regularly in the press. The controversial "Team B" intelligence estimate of Soviet strategic capabilities and intentions, purposely leaked, concluded that the Soviet Union would soon pass the United States in almost every major military category.[63] Alarms about civil defense efforts in the Soviet Union were regularly sounded; such activities, it was claimed, showed the enemy's aim for superiority. In a national television interview Stansfield Turner, the new CIA director, warned of an eroding military balance. The Russians, he said, "by building a military force that they hope will weigh in the balance for them," were trying to compensate for other weaknesses.[64]

With this steady dose of warnings about the Soviet Union's military activities, the American public was not inclined to favor cuts in defense. A December 1976 survey by the Opinion Research Corporation of Princeton, New Jersey, said a majority wanted "a stronger defense," while a Harris survey found nearly two out of every three people wanting to keep defense spending around current levels or to increase it somewhat.[65] A Cadell poll covering a similar period showed the public wanting increased federal spending in, first, aid to the elderly; then health care, education, crime and drug-abuse prevention, social security, air- and water-pollution control, and aid to the handicapped; and, finally, an adequate national defense.[66]

International events, however, can swiftly change Congress's course. The House Budget Committee reported its First Concurrent Resolution on March 30, 1977, with a reduction from the level requested by Carter of $4 billion in budget authority and $2 billion in outlays. The committee's new chairman, Robert Giaimo, emphasized savings in inflation accounts in operations and maintenance and in foreign military sales trust fund and stockpile sales, as well as personnel and compensation reforms.[67] The Senate Budget Committee was preparing a similar resolution, but the day before the committee's mark-up began, Secretary of State Cyrus Vance left the Moscow SALT negotiations empty-handed. Congress's response was to close ranks. Minority Leader Howard Baker said in the Senate, "I hope the world understands that while we have Republicans and Democrats in Congress and in the country, we have only one President, and in the matter of testing we will stand firmly and squarely behind our President, as he is now challenged or may later be challenged."[68] Majority Leader Robert Byrd reiterated the president's warning: "If no agreement should be forthcoming, the United States would be forced to consider a much more deep commitment to the development and deployment of additional weapons."[69] Muskie, Ernest Hollings, and Biden privately agreed not to cut defense allocations. Indeed, at Hollings' urging, the Budget Committee added $300 million in budget authority to the purchases account; some reductions were made in the manpower area. Hollings cited the need "to improve readiness and provide for increased forces and to signal to the Soviets our intention to respond to the breakdown in the SALT talks."[70]

Thus the two committees reported out different defense spending levels, with the House cutting in management areas, the Senate stepping up weapons programs and improving readiness in response to the recent SALT failure.[71]

Some members of Congress feared that the Soviet Union would make no concessions to end the SALT impasse, but would simply wait for the United States to alter its position as they believed the United States had done in the past. Furthermore, in his first half-year in office, President Carter had reversed or modified his public position on several controversial issues, such as the $50 tax rebate, the "hit list" of federal water projects, his initial plan for low farm price supports. It was believed on Capitol Hill that the Russians would expect a comparable softening on SALT if they held out long enough. Cautious senators, wanting the United States to hold firm, relayed that message to Carter and to the Soviet Union by voting for military readiness.

The process temporarily broke down on the House floor because of the Budget Committee's $116 billion defense target. Maximalists, arguing for executive supremacy in national security matters, won passage of an amendment restoring moneys the committee had cut.[72] "The restoration does not reflect any expertise on the part of Omar Burleson," the amendment's author, "but it does reflect the judgment of the President of the United States and the opinion of the Department of Defense, and the [Office of Management and Budget]."[73] Telephone calls from the president and the secretary of defense to congressmen as well as a letter from Secretary Brown to Burleson had helped the maximalists. Congressman Melvin Price, chairman of the Armed Services Committee, said the budget process "is not going to work if national defense is going to be made the whipping boy for those who want to spend money in other areas or try out favorite theories on economic stimulation."[74]

The Budget Committee was distressed. The Burleson Amendment had broken "the delicate balance," Giaimo contended, "between defense and domestic spending proposed by the Budget Committee." House Democrats opposed the amendment 164 to 106, but Republicans supported it 119 to 20, with members of the Armed Services Committee and Republicans providing the necessary margin. Giaimo charged the president with trying to "dictate" to Congress. "This is the United States Congress. It is not the Georgia legislature," he said.[75] Speaker O'Neill chided Carter and Brown for having "made an end-around play" on the budget issue, "not knowing the ways of Congress," which "kind of fouled things up."[76]

Nonetheless, liberal, moderate, and southern Democrats, plus all but two Republicans, voted 320 to 84 against the First Budget Resolution. Two days later, the Budget Committee approved a "compromise" by voice vote. It included reduced amounts for programs that previously had been added to, in particular $1.15 billion in budget authority and $300 million in outlays for defense. Giaimo said the reworked resolution attempted to "strike a balance between defense and nondefense spending" acceptable to a majority in the House.[77] Just before floor consideration, Majority Leader Jim Wright urged Democrats not to repeat the previous week's mistakes and add moneys to the resolution that would make it politically impossible to pass. If this happened, the legislative branch, he warned, would "be the victim of a self-imposed paralysis."[78]

At a White House meeting Muskie told President Carter and the cabinet, "Once the process is viewed as an adjunct of the executive branch it will be done in." O'Neill said that the defense secretary was "expected to mind his own business." He pointed out, "There was a chain of command in the Defense Department and a chain of command in the House. We need the budget resolution to function."[79] The resolution passed 213 (including seven Republican votes) to 179; four attempts to raise the defense spending target above the level recommended by the committee were defeated.[80] Wright thought "the presence of the budget process, the integrity of Congress and the capacity to have a budget and control spending took priority."[81] In short, preserving an internal institution took precedence over following the lead of the executive branch.

At the Senate-House conference on the First Budget Resolution for Fiscal 1978, defense spending was the central issue. Only $3.2 billion in budget authority and $1.7 billion in outlays separated the two houses, but the gap represented political symbols that proved tough to overcome. A contest developed between defense and social spending priorities, not the proper level of funding for a strong United States defense. The Senate's targets of $120.3 billion in budget authority and $111.6 billion in outlays represented a stand against the Soviet Union, a desire to strengthen NATO, and reelection worries. These factors were "not as visible" as they were in the House,

Muskie explained, but if the Senate conferees brought back too low a total for defense spending, it would be hard to hold the Senate to it.[82] The House Democratic conferees were determined to maintain a balance in overall spending. Otherwise, political polarization in the lower chamber would make it impossible to pass the Budget Resolution. "The overwhelming majority of first- and second-term members," Giaimo told the conference, "feel that for years we have gone along and rubber-stamped defense requests and as a result deprived ourselves of monies that we needed in other areas. . . . They feel very strongly and they are a large number . . .; they are 53 percent of the Democratic majority in the House.[83] . . . The issue here is the untouchableness of the defense budget." The newer members resent the Pentagon's "efforts to hold us absolutely to the line." They want to see some indication that the Defense Department is "going to participate in sharing the burden of high deficits and unavailability of money in many areas."[84]

Hollings admitted that there was no magic number for the military. "If you get a strong SALT agreement and President Carter comes back and cuts 7 billion, we could cut 7 billion perhaps." But "if he came back here, and he said SALT is really gone . . . we ought to add 7, I think we could get the 7." He stressed how important it was to address the issues as stated in the Senate report rather than let the issue be the "liberal Democrats" in the House. "We address the Soviets and the build-up."[85] He also pointed to the electoral connection currently at work in the Senate. This was why, he said, Senator Thomas Eagleton had not offered his amendment in the Senate to cut more from the Budget Committee's defense level. No one offered an amendment. For a while, senators had believed that cutting the defense budget would win them votes back home. But the tide had turned: the minimalists "all of a sudden have gotten lockjaw."[86]

On the third day of the deadlocked conference, still seeking "a number I can enforce," Muskie met privately with Stennis and McClellan to arrive at a consensus of the key Senate chairmen on the appropriate defense target. They agreed to $118.5 billion in budget authority and $111 billion in outlays (the Senate targets had been $120.3 and $111.6 billion respectively), with the stipulation that the reductions were not to come from research and development or procurement of new weapons. Muskie then caucused with his own conferees, telling them he had gone to the two "people who determine the defense spending environment on the Senate floor." He wanted, he said, to prevent the budget process from "foundering," as it had in the 1940s at this phase. He said Stennis, too, "wanted the process to hold up" and accepted the adjusted amounts. Hollings feared the cuts went too far. "Are we all going to hang together?" he asked. But when the other maximalist Senate conferees accepted the compromise, he went along.[87] Muskie then conveyed the offer informally to Giaimo, who then caucused with the House conferees.

When the conference reassembled, Muskie formally submitted the compromise motion, specifying where Congress wanted the savings to come: "This substitute assumes that financial adjustments can be made to the administration's budget request in order to remain within these targets. Such adjustments may include a possible slowdown in projected foreign military sales; the utilization of prior-year unobligated funds to finance a portion of the Fiscal Year 1978 program; a lower inflation rate from that now assumed in the administration's budget; and a partial absorption of the October pay raise."[88] An overwhelming majority of conferees approved the compromise, in Muskie's words, "in the interest of preserving and promoting the Congressional budget process."[89]

Politics of the Purse

The Congressional Budget and Impoundment Control Act has strengthened the legislative branch. In implementing the act, Congress has begun the long, difficult process of reclaiming equal footing in formulating overall defense policy and analyzing fundamental issues.

Until 1975 the legislative branch exercised the power of the purse in piecemeal fashion, responding one by one to presidential spending requests. Members considered each military spending measure on its political merits but rarely in relation to total federal spending. This made Congress a dependent of the administration; it had effectively conceded the power of the purse, the ultimate constraint on policymaking, to the executive branch.

In changing the way Congress looks at key defense issues, the Budget Act has strengthened Congress's hold on the purse strings. Decisions must be mathematically consistent and coherent with regard to total budget authority, outlays, revenues, public debt levels, and the budget surplus or deficit. Annual appropriations and spending authority for each federal program, including national defense, must now be at or fall below the ceilings Congress itself establishes. Consequently, defense spending has become part of the total budget framework; choices can be made with reference to other areas of expenditure, as well as within the defense area.

Congress does not debate a separate military budget each January; nor will it do so in the foreseeable future. But Congress is no longer the government orphan, excluded from information or program analysis and evaluation. While basic data still come from the executive branch, Congress is now capable of scrutinizing and challenging those data as well as the assumptions underlying defense plans and programs. Furthermore, Congress can now look beyond the pork barrel to appraise end purposes, focusing first on what the money is being requested for and why it is needed—and then on how it is to be spent.

The Senate Budget Committee has tried to use a mission budget for defense expenditures in Fiscal 1977 and 1978. In Fiscal 1979 the budget act required mission budgets for all government agencies; the Senate Committee utilized its own mission cost model that provided an unprecedented overall view of military spending, on the basis of which Congress can determine priorities both among defense missions and between defense and other areas of federal spending. Spurred by the Budget Committee, the Senate Armed Services Committee tried using a mission format for a few of its Fiscal 1978 hearings; this methodology identified a reason for the diminishing United States lead in technology. "The temptation [is] to try to manage the details of a specific program," the committee stated, "rather than wrestle with the more complex issues of policy and direction for our national defense posture. . . . The net result is not enough emphasis on the major policy issues and too much emphasis on detailed project management.''[90]

The new budget process provides an open and modern means of allocating resources among competing national needs, of deciding which activities have priority, which should be carried out by the federal government, and how they should be financed. After three years' experience, members of the Budget Committees are now weighing the value of improved military preparedness against improved health and welfare measures and the development of new sources of energy.

Implicit in this whole process is a rejection of the status quo. First, to be powerful and to sustain the "institutionalized mutuality" of responsible coequals,[91] Congress must be buttressed with knowledge. Independent sources of information are indispensable to the formulation of intelligent alternative policies, especially when Congress disagrees with the executive over the direction policy should take.[92] Congress "can violently disturb, but it cannot often fathom, the waters of the sea in which the bigger fish of the civil service swim and feed," wrote Woodrow Wilson in *Congressional Government*.[93] To fathom the waters in which the gigantic fish of the defense establishment feed, Congress requires its own base of information and analysis. This is being provided by the relatively large professional staffs of the two Budget Committees and the Congressional Budget Office. Congress still defers to executive initiatives on weapons systems, but as the debates over defense expenditures for Fiscal 1977 and 1978 showed, this is due not to docile acquiescence toward executive requests, but to a congressional consensus favoring competition with the Soviet Union in weapons build-ups. Through the new budget process more information is collected, assembled, and analyzed, and many more usable alternatives for defense spending decisions are presented than at any time in the history of Congress. More information produces more questions; the more information is shared, the more power is too, which is the intent of the Constitution.

Second, the process is imposing on Congress a long-term— i.e., five- to ten-year—look at federal programs. This points up the need for advanced budgeting. One apparently small decision for the fiscal year under debate can ramify for years. Examples are the decision not to reform military retirement, to procure the M-X ICBM, to allow the Navy to build vessels for both the power projection and sea control missions, to keep 2.1 million people in the active forces because that is the current level. It was evaluation of the B-1's long-term consequences, in a series, by Congress and then by the new president and his defense secretary, that eventually led to the airplane's demise. The congressional budget process cannot come fully of age, however, until the long-range spending impact of all major items in the current budget is carefully explored and exposed.

The electoral connection does not necessarily impede sound decision making. Political judgments are an essential aspect of policy decisions. Indeed, it is Congress's prime responsibility to use the power of the purse to make such judgments. Senators and representatives will continue to look out for their constituents' interests and their own careers. The challenge is to broaden those interests in a way that enriches the decision-making process and strengthens Congress. The new budget process, in contrast to the authorization and appropriations processes, focuses a member's attention beyond his immediate constituency to the nation as a whole. By concerning itself with the wisdom of defense policies as well as efficiency and expense, Congress has reclaimed some power over the purse. In defining its goal as providing maximum strength within the limits of the nation's economic means, Congress is exercising a new degree of influence over military policy; for the means it makes available to pursue the nation's ends will largely determine what ends can be pursued.

Budget control thus gives Congress a greater managerial voice in major military matters.[94] And arms management is potentially a form of arms control. The process invites Congress to concentrate on the relationship between spending and the size and content of the national arsenal. To date the new budget process has not been used to limit weaponry or manpower in the name of arms control. Additional costs have been voted with the intent to strengthen the military; reductions have been based on fiscal prudence. No old nuclear weapons systems have been eliminated. Proposals for a new strategic system have not been developed, banned, or traded off against conventional military programs. But at least the capability for such decisions now exists, and the renewed vigor and expertise of Congress suggest that it may be exercised.

As was shown in the debates on defense spending in Fiscal 1977 and 1978, arms control requires a receptive political environment. The new budget process can only be as powerful as the majority in Congress wills it to be. Answering such questions as—How much is enough? Which missions require this weapon, on the basis of what policy? What is the United States really trying to defend?—requires skepticism toward the status quo, hard work and long-term planning, and deliberate exercise of the power of the purse.

In reforming its own ways and strengthening its own means, Congress is reclaiming its Constitutional role in the governance of foreign and defense policy. A degree of equilibrium in legislative-executive relations has been restored by the institution of new budget procedures and the discipline they impose. Both houses are now equipped with the analytical and technical means to meet the executive head on, even to initiate or enact alternative military policies, for the first time since the dawning of the nuclear age. "The challenge now, with a President and a Congressional majority of the same party," Muskie has said, "is to insure that the Congressional [budget] process does work and continues to work as a separate, independent process, with an integrity of its own, a policy-making potential of its own, a data-accumulation base of its own, so that we will be in a position to assert our responsibilities under the Constitution over the power of the purse."[95]

Notes

1. U.S., Congress, House, Committee on Appropriations, *Hearings: National Military Establishment Appropriations Bill for 1950*, 81st Cong., 2d sess., pp. 5, 14.

2. See Les Aspin, "The Defense Budget and Foreign Policy: The Role of Congress," *Daedalus* 104 (Summer 1975): 155-174; Robert S. Benson, "The Military on Capitol Hill: Prospects in the Quest

for Funds," *The Annals of the American Academy of Political and Social Science,* March 1973, pp. 48-58; Committee for Economic Development, *Congressional Decision-Making for National Security* (New York, 1974).

3. Katherine Johnsen, "Support for B-1 Decision Seen Mixed in Congress," *Aviation Week & Space Technology,* July 11, 1977, pp. 21-22.

4. Edward J. Laurance, in "The Changing Role of Congress in Defense Policy-Making," *Journal of Conflict Resolution* 20 (June 1976): 213-53, offers quantitative evidence that Congress increased its role between 1967 and 1974. In his conclusion, however, Laurance recognizes, "To the extent that we are dissatisfied with the current defense policy system, we must look for a reform of the Congressional system as a whole."

5. Edwin S. Corwin, *The President: Office and Powers,* rev. ed. (New York, 1957), p. 171.

6. Congressional Budget and Impoundment Control Act of 1974, Pub. L. no. 344, 88 Stat. 297, *codified at* 31 U.S.C.A. secs. 1301 *et seq.* (Supp. 1975).

7. Aspin, "The Defense Budget and Foreign Policy," p. 163.

8. Julius Allen, "New Process Offers Lid on Arms Costs," *SANEWorld,* November 1975.

9. Bernard Brodie, "On the Objectives of Arms Control," *International Security* 1 (Summer 1976): 19.

10. Public Law 86-149 was amended in 1959 and expanded in 1962, 1963, 1965, 1967, 1969, 1970, 1972, and 1973. U.S., Congress, Senate, Committee on Armed Services, *Report on the Activities of the Committee on Armed Services,* 93rd Cong., Senate Rept. 94-95, (1975), pp. 6-8. These enactments were codified by Section 803(a) of PL 93-155 into Title 10, U.S. Code, as Section 138. On the Armed Services Committee's jurisdictional gains in the Russell-Stennis era, see Nancy J. Bearg and Edwin A. Deagle, Jr., "Congress and the Defense Budget," in *American Defense Policy,* ed. John E. Endicott and Roy W. Stafford, Jr. (Baltimore, 1977).

11. Albert G. Dancy, Sr., "Effects of Congressional Funding Limitations on Development of Major Defense Systems," *Armed Forces Comptroller,* October 1976, pp. 24-27; Craig Liske and Barry Runquist, *The Politics of Weapons Procurement: The Role of Congress* (Denver, 1974).

12. For previous attempts by Congress to control spending as well as the history of the current effort, see Allen Schick, "The Battle of the Budget," in *Congress against the President,* ed. Harvey Mansfield,

Sr. (New York, 1975).

13. J. Ronald Fox, *Arming America: How the U.S. Buys Weapons* (Boston, 1974), pp. 125, 128. See also Berkeley Rice, *The C-5A Scandal* (Boston, 1971).

14. Quoted in Samuel P. Huntington, *The Common Defense* (New York, 1961), p. 135.

15. See Daniel Yergin, "The Arms Zealots," *Harper's,* June 1977, pp. 64-76, on the beliefs and history of the maximalists, or "arms coalition lobby," and its perennial struggle with the minimalists, or "arms control lobby," over the direction of U.S. policy toward the Soviet Union. Yergin expands on his thesis in *Shattered Peace: The Origins of the Cold War and the National Security State* (Boston, 1977). See also Elizabeth Drew, "An Argument Over Survival," *The New Yorker,* April 4, 1977, pp. 99-117, for a careful rundown of the debate in Washington over the early Carter SALT policy.

16. Quoted in Fox, *Arming America,* p. 138.

17. George C. Wilson, "Battle Lines Drawn on Defense Research," *Washington Post* (hereafter *Wash. Post),* March 15, 1971.

18. Fox, *Arming America,* p. 124. See also pp. 140-51 for detailed discussion of congressional behavior at defense budget hearings.

19. Letter from Elmer B. Staats, comptroller general of the United States, to Senator William L. Scott, June 10, 1977, inserted in *Congressional Record* (hereafter *Congr. Rec.),* July 26, 1977, S-12796.

20. John W. Allsbrook, "Role of Congressional Staffs in Weapon System Acquisition," *Defense Systems Management Review* 1 (Spring 1977): 34-41.

21. David R. Mayhew, *Congress: The Electoral Connection* (New Haven, Conn., 1974), pp. 5, 121-24.

22. Ibid., p. 122.

23. Liske and Runquist, *The Politics of Weapons Procurement,* p. 91.

24. Aaron Wildavsky, *The Politics of the Budgetry Process* (Boston, 1964).

25. U.S., Department of Defense, *Annual Defense Department Report: FY 1976,* 94th Cong., 1st sess., February 5, 1975.

26. Speech given in Washington, D.C., January 27, 1976. Cranston's support of the California-based B-1 bomber demonstrates that minimalist defense spenders are not immune to constituency pressures.

27. Letter from Chiles to Muskie, March 10, 1975.

28. U.S., Congress, House, Committee on the Budget, *Hearings: Force Structure and Long-Range Projections,* vols. 1 and 2, 94th

Cong., 1st sess., September 1975.

29. A special staff work group under the direction of Samuel H. Cohn, *1976 Budget Alternatives and Analyses: Report to the Committees on the Budget of the U.S. Congress,* April 15, 1975, pp. 67-80.

30. U.S., Congress, Senate, Committee on the Budget, *Report: First Concurrent Resolution on the Budget—Fiscal Year 1976,* 94th Cong., S. Rept. 94-77, April 15, 1975, p. 129.

31. *Congr. Rec.,* April 29, 1975, S-7067.

32. Letter from Muskie and Bellmon to all senators, July 30, 1975.

33. *Congr. Rec.,* August 1, 1975, S-14719.

34. Letter of July 29, 1975.

35. Statement of July 25, 1975.

36. *Congr. Rec.,* August 1, 1975, S-14723. During the appropriations phase of the process, McClellan kept his promise to hold the Defense Appropriations bill within the resolution.

37. Ibid., S-14721.

38. Ibid., S-14725-26.

39. Senate Budget Committee Memorandum, Tom Dine to Douglas Bennet and John McEvoy, October 1, 1975. See also statement by Senators Cranston, Eagleton, Hatfield, Kennedy, Mathias, Proxmire, and Schweiker, October 20, 1975, and subsequent news articles; Senate Budget Committee Memorandum, Dine to Muskie, October 23, 1975; Speech by Senator Sam Nunn, *Congr. Rec.,* October 29, 1975, S-18920-22.

40. John Finney, "Bipartisan Bloc in Senate Fights to Cut Arms Fund," *New York Times,* October 20, 1975.

41. Statement of October 19, 1975.

42. George C. Wilson, "Pentagon Tactics Resented on Hill," *Wash. Post,* October 26, 1975.

43. McClellan to Muskie, October 8, 1975; Muskie and Bellmon to McClellan, October 22, 1975.

44. "Unexpectedly, Pentagon Loses a Budget Battle," *N.Y. Times,* November 2, 1975, and John Finney, "Defense Fund Cut Voted in Senate," ibid., November 7, 1975.

45. Richard L. Madden, "Congress Succeeding on Spending Checks," ibid., December 13, 1975.

46. George C. Wilson, "Pentagon Cashes In," *Wash. Post,* May 15, 1976.

47. U.S., Office of Management and Budget, *The Budget of the United States Government, Fiscal Year 1977,* January 21, 1976, pp. 61-79.

48. U.S., Department of Defense, *Annual Defense Department Report: FY 1977*, 94th Cong., 2d sess., January 27, 1976.

49. Drew Middleton, "Thinking About the Thinkable: Politics and the Arms Race," *Atlantic*, August 1976, p. 57.

50. Thomas A. Dine, Robert D. Sneed, and Robin Pirie, "U.S./U.S.S.R. Military Spending," March 3, 1976, published in U.S., Congress, Committee on the Budget, *Budget Issues: Staff Studies for Fiscal 1977*, 94th Cong., 2d sess., June 28, 1976, pp. 127-65.

51. Ibid., p. 142.

52. Wilson, *Wash. Post*, May 15, 1976.

53. Unpublished transcript of mark-up session, p. 205.

54. Kenneth H. Bacon, "Reagan and the Defense Issue," *Wall Street Journal*, June 7, 1976.

55. Unpublished transcript of mark-up session, pp. 185-86; *Wash. Post*, May 15, 1976.

56. Speech of April 4, 1976.

57. *N.Y. Times*, April 5, 1976.

58. U.S., Congress, Senate, *Amendments to the 1977 Appropriations Requested for the Department of Defense*, 94th Cong., 2d sess., S. Doc. 94-186, May 10, 1976.

59. *Aviation Week & Space Technology*, October 18, 1976, p. 13.

60. William Watts and Lloyd A. Free, "Nationalism, Not Isolationism," *Foreign Policy* 24 (Fall 1976): 5.

61. Statement of October 1976.

62. U.S., Congress, Senate, Committee on the Budget, *Hearings on the First Concurrent Resolution on the Budget—Fiscal Year 1978*, vol. 1, 94th Cong., 1st sess., pp. 55-56.

63. David Binder, "New C.I.A. Estimate Finds Soviet Seeks Superiority in Arms," *N.Y. Times*, December 26, 1976; David Binder, "The West's Defense Debate," *European Community*, May-June 1977.

64. "CIA Director Sees Military Balance Eroding," *Aviation Week & Space Technology*, March 28, 1977, p. 17.

65. Insert by Senator Barry Goldwater in *Congr. Rec.*, February 1, 1977, S-1975; Louis Harris, "Most Don't Favor Cuts in Defense," *Chicago Tribune*, January 17, 1977.

66. Insert by Congressman Claude Pepper in *Congr. Rec.*, May 13, 1977, H-4432.

67. U.S., Congress, House, Committee on the Budget, *Report of the First Concurrent Resolution—FY 1978*, 95th Cong., 1st sess., April 6, 1977, pp. 26-30.

68. *Congr. Rec.*, March 31, 1977, S-5225.

69. Ibid., S-5226.

70. U.S., Congress, Senate, Committee on the Budget, *Report of the First Concurrent Resolution for FY 1978* 95th Cong., 1st sess., April 12, 1977, p. 32.

71. On Senate ambiguity and House line-iteming, see James L. Rowe, Jr., "Hill's Budget Committees Differ on Their Approaches, Priorities," *Wash. Post,* April 12, 1977.

72. *Congr. Rec.,* April 27, 1977, H-3625-92.

73. Ibid., H-3627.

74. Ibid., H-3643.

75. Giaimo statement of April 28, 1977; Adam Clymer, "House Democrats Angry Over Defeat of Budget Plan," *N.Y. Times,* April 29, 1977. See also "Blundering on the Budget," editorial, ibid., May 3, 1977.

76. James L. Rowe, Jr., "House Sends Budget Resolution Back to Panel," *Wash. Post,* April 29, 1977.

77. James L. Rowe, Jr., "House Panel Trims Down '78 Budget, Compromises on Defense and Deficit," ibid., April 30, 1977.

78. Adam Clymer, "Budget Ceiling Vote Worries House Chief," *N.Y. Times,* May 5, 1977.

79. Ron Sarro, "Democrats Seeking Loyalty to House Budget Panel," *Washington Star,* May 5, 1977.

80. *Congr. Rec.,* May 5, 1977, H-4064-110.

81. James L. Rowe, Jr., "House Votes Compromise Budget Target," *Wash. Post,* May 6, 1977.

82. U.S., Congress, Conference of the Committees on the Budget, unpublished transcript of May 10-11, 1977, p. 139.

83. Ibid., p. 172.

84. Ibid., p. 162.

85. Ibid., p. 183.

86. Ibid., p. 124.

87. Author's notes, Caucus of Senate Conferees, May 11, 1977.

88. Budget Committees' conference transcript, May 10-11, p. 250; U.S., Congress, Senate, Conference Rept. 95-134, 95th Cong., 1st sess., May 11, 1977, p. 6.

89. *Congr. Rec.,* May 11, 1977, S-7440. Two Republican House conferees signed the report, the first time any GOP House Budget Committee member had done so. Congresswoman Majorie Holt then rounded up 28 for passage on the floor. "If we [Republicans] hope to influence the budget process," she said, "then we must be part of the process. . . . Like they say over in our lottery in Maryland, 'You gotta play to win.' " *Congr. Rec.,* May 17, 1977, H-4559-60.

90. U.S., Congress, Senate, Committee on Armed Services, 95th Cong., 1st sess., S. Rept. 95-129, May 10, 1977.

91. Ernest S. Griffith, *Congress: Its Contemporary Role,* 4th ed. (New York, 1967), p. 7.

92. Thomas A. Dine, "A Primer for Capitol Hill," *N.Y. Times,* April 4, 1975.

93. Quoted in Griffith, *Congress,* p. 46.

94. J. A. Stockfisch, *Plowshares into Swords: Managing the American Defense Establishment* (New York, 1973).

95. *Congr. Rec.,* February 21, 1977, S-2804.

5

The Foreign Relations Committee and the Future of Arms Control

Dick Clark

There is every reason to believe that the congressional session of 1977-78 is going to be marked by the most significant arms control debate since the SALT I Interim Agreement. In the period following that agreement in 1972, there was remarkably little public debate of the issues, largely because observers were waiting patiently for the follow-up negotiations. Only the Backfire and cruise missile problems received any attention at all, and much of that was demagogic. And when the Vladivostok agreements were finally achieved, the United States was well into a presidential election campaign that never really focused properly on arms control.

My confidence that we are facing a thoroughgoing debate persists despite an awareness that SALT II deadlocked following the presentation of President Carter's new proposals in Moscow last March. Without examining the merits of the March proposals, let me observe that since they represented the first initiative incorporating meaningful quantitative reductions and qualitative controls, it was inevitable that they would be controversial in both Washington and Moscow. The comprehensive package provision permitting the Soviet Union an aggregate throw weight advantage, i. e., an overall payload advantage, of about 4:1 has already touched off a heated debate in Washington; and both the proposed limits on heavy missiles and the lowering of the overall Vladivostok ICBM totals—

which drew no response from the Soviets in Moscow—will likely fuel the controversy within the Soviet establishment.

But quite aside from the Moscow package, there are several other issues that will force the debate. President Carter's decision not to proceed with the B-1 bomber, laudable as it was, also compels a detailed national debate on the future course of American strategy. As euphoria over the B-1 cancellation wanes, many persons are realizing that the president may have opened a Pandora's box of new weaponry. At the very least, the decision injects the cruise missile into a central strategic role, with arms control ramifications we are just beginning to discern. Moreover, the B-1 decision is also being used to justify construction of the MX missile in a mobile mode, with control and verification problems of enormous complexity.

In anticipation of the coming debate, it is illuminating to ask how the various political elements involved will act, in particular the Senate Foreign Relations Committee. In this regard the congressional track experience in handling the nomination of Paul Warnke to be director of the Arms Control and Disarmament Agency (ACDA) and head of the SALT negotiating team offers us a useful guide.

The Warnke nomination was seen quite correctly, I believe, by both the arms control community and its opponents as a signal of the president's determination to proceed energetically with arms control. Thus the confirmation debate—frequently vitriolic and bitter—tended to focus as much on personal arms control philosophies as on Warnke's qualifications.

Formal jurisdiction for the Warnke nomination lay with the Foreign Relations Committee, where, with a couple of exceptions, Warnke got a positive reception. Within the committee the widespread opinion was held that for the first time since Gerard Smith headed ACDA, the administration would be taking its cue on arms control issues from somebody who actually believed in arms control as a vital aspect of national security. Despite the many charges and attacks against Mr. Warnke, the Foreign Relations Committee's ten Democrats and six Republicans voted for him by a 15-1 margin as ACDA head, and 14-2 as leader of the SALT delegation.

The real differences that prevail in Washington on arms

control and defense matters surfaced when the Armed Services Committee, although technically without jurisdiction, held "informal" hearings, calling Warnke as well as several hostile witnesses, notably Paul Nitze and Admiral Thomas Moorer, to testify. The arms control "hawks"—led by Senator Henry Jackson—made every effort to maneuver Mr. Warnke into an impossibly narrow position on verification. They did get him to say that an unverifiable agreement is worse than none at all. However, it was a stand-off on what constitutes "adequate" verification. But Nitze had to concede a flexible interpretation of verification that really conceded very little. He said:

> I have always taken the position that the significance of verification is to be related to the significance of the thing you are verifying. If it is not very important it doesn't make that much difference. In other words, it is the product of the strategic importance of the things being limited and the verifiability of the limitation which is important, not just absolute verifiability.

This, too, can be read in many ways—which is true of most of the discussion on verification. But it is evident that the verification issue will be at the center of the debate over any SALT II agreement.

In addition, although the confirmation of Harold Brown as secretary of defense was not within the jursidiction of the Foreign Relations Committee, within that committee his nomination was strongly favored. Most members felt that Brown is precisely the sort of person who can bridge differences between doctrinaire military hard-liners and arms control advocates. His broad experience, particularly in Robert McNamara's Pentagon and as secretary of the Air Force, makes him relatively invulnerable to charges of "softness," while at the same time he is outspokenly critical of those who believe a nuclear war can be "won."

The Warnke and Brown appointments, it seems to me, are evidence that the Carter administration is determined to introduce a new momentum to arms control. The president's new arms transfer doctrine, the Moscow SALT II proposals, and the decision on the B-1 all confirm that this is indeed his intention. And ultimately, this policy will be scrutinized first and foremost by the Senate Foreign Relations Committee.

The General Background

Before probing current developments more closely, let us review the basic responsibilities of the Foreign Relations Committee in the arms control field.

The committee has jurisdiction over general arms control and disarmament matters, arms sales, treaties, executive agreements, and military and economic assistance programs. It also oversees the operations and activities of the Department of State and ACDA, and works closely with both agencies. Under Senate Resolution 4, which reorganized Senate committee jurisdictions in 1976, the committee's responsibility was extended to the international aspects of nuclear energy, including nuclear transfer policy, an area previously covered by the Joint Atomic Energy Committee. The Foreign Relations Committee was also given the charter to "study and review, on a comprehensive basis, matters relating to the national security policy . . . of the United States."

Obviously, just how the committee carries out these functions depends in part on its relationship to the administration. As it has demonstrated repeatedly, the committee, although basically supportive of President Carter, often expresses views somewhat different from those of his administration. Hence there was considerable opposition to the B-1 in the committee even when the president was thought to be leaning toward limited production of it, and opposition to the so-called enhanced radiation warhead as well. Arms transfer decisions by the executive are often questioned, although until now none has been disapproved. The closest the committee came to overturning such a transfer was on the AWACS (Airborne Warning and Control System) sale to Iran, where a compromise was negotiated by the administration with the committee in the summer of 1977.

We will now look at the three major areas of arms control activity—SALT, conventional arms sales, and nuclear proliferation—in terms of what has been accomplished recently, and what may reasonably be expected to come before the Foreign Relations Committee.

SALT

Congressional involvement in SALT since the 1972 ratification of the Treaty Limiting Anti-Ballistic Missile Systems and the Interim Agreement on Offensive Arms has been low-key, largely, as noted earlier, because of the expectation that the Interim Agreement would be converted into a treaty that the Foreign Relations Committee would then consider. The Interim Agreement—a five-year restriction on further deployment of strategic offensive missile launchers—was always viewed as a somewhat less than satisfactory makeshift arrangement until negotiators could achieve a more complete limitation on strategic offensive arms.

However, growing congressional frustration with the pace of negotiations produced an effort in March 1976 to accelerate the talks. Senators Edward Kennedy, Jacob Javits, Hubert Humphrey, myself, and others urged the president to propose to the Soviets a ban on flight testing and deployment by either country of land- or sea-launched cruise missiles with a range greater than 600 kilometers, and air-launched cruise missiles with a range greater than 2,500 kilometers. We wanted to try to avoid letting the cruise missile genie out of the bottle, as had happened with the deployment of MIRVs. The effort was not received kindly by the Ford administration. The only response was a sharply critical press conference by then ACDA director Fred Iklé.

The returns are not yet in on whether the Carter administration will look more favorably than its predecessor on congressional involvement in SALT. Secretary of State Cyrus Vance and ACDA head Paul Warnke both assured the Foreign Relations Committee during confirmation hearings that they would keep the members fully informed on the negotiations' progress. Before going to Moscow in early 1977, Secretary Vance appeared before the committee in executive session to provide an extremely detailed briefing on the planned proposals to the Soviet Union. Subsequently, he returned at several stages to report to the committee. This has been informative, although of limited utility, because the committee is being told of decisions already taken, rather than consulted as the American position evolves. I and others on the committee have doubts about the wisdom of the approach taken in the Moscow package, and possibly if we had been consulted at an earlier stage, some of the more obvious difficulties might have been avoided. If the administration expects effective support from committee members when the SALT II agreement comes to the Senate floor, it is imperative that officials have cooperated to the fullest extent throughout the negotiations.

For their part the members of the committee have made extraordinary effort to prepare for the technicalities of a possible SALT II agreement. For example, I have launched my own "Operation SALT," which involves returning to first assumptions and reviewing both the substance and the personalities of the entire SALT negotiations. As part of this project, I have had private conversations in my office with Ambassadors Gerard Smith and U. Alexis Johnson, and a host of former or present members of the SALT negotiating team, including Warnke. A comprehensive reading program has been set up to provide the necessary technical background. Several other members have been following a similar schedule.

Whatever course SALT takes, several valid generalizations can be made about the sentiment of the Foreign Relations Committee:

1. There is strong consensus within the committee in favor of a strategic arms control agreement. Details aside, the committee endorses the general direction the president has proposed.

2. The committee will scrutinize any agreement for loopholes or loosely drawn provisions. While most of the members do not accept the allegations that the USSR has cheated on SALT I or violated its provisions, it is clear to us that the Soviets exploit every possible advantage. Furthermore, the issuance of unilateral clarifying declarations has been thoroughly discredited. Fortunately, Warnke has made it clear that he also sees little point in having recourse to this device.

3. The central issue of the coming debate on SALT II will be verification, rather than the numbers themselves or other features of the accord. A brief review of the Warnke nomination hearings makes it clear that the critics of an accord believe they can scuttle the whole thing on the issue of verification. Verification clearly is a relative term. What most of us mean is not absolute security, but adequate assurance that the risk, which is always present, is acceptable. But it is an issue subject to considerable demagoguery and posturing. With this in mind, a group of us amended the Arms Control and Disarmament Act in 1977 to reaffirm our support for verification but to blunt the demand for total verification by emphasizing the qualifier "adequate." As I warned on the floor of the Senate at the time, "Nevertheless, there is a point where the search for perfect verification becomes its own end and agreements which can be adequately verified are lost in argumentation over how to attain complete, 100 percent confidence." That amendment passed the Senate, but its support by opponents of a SALT agreement emphasizes that the showdown battle is still shrouded in semantics. When the final agreement comes to the Senate, the differing interpretations of "adequate" verification will obviously be a major point of contention.

4. At some point we are going to have to confront the question of the Soviet civil defense capability, if only because some American observers argue that it could make the Soviets think they could survive a nuclear exchange with less than total devastation. In that regard civil defense could in theory become a kind of substitute for ABM. Expert witnesses before the committee in recent hearings on the Triad have rejected claims that the Soviets have a system that could affect the strategic balance. But a concentrated civil defense effort by the Soviets leads many Americans to believe they have such a capability. And so the committee probably will encourage the extension of SALT into that area. There should be no difficulty with the administration over this; Warnke agreed fully with this view during his confirmation hearings.

5. It is impossible to predict just how the committee will decide on the issue of the Backfire and cruise missiles. It

is unfortunate that these two systems should have become equated in the public mind, for they are really quite disparate. Linking cruise missiles and Backfire was accidental; they were merely the two major unresolved remnants of the 1974 Vladivostok talks. In my view, it would be far wiser to deal with both the cruise and Backfire issues in the SALT II settlement rather than leaving them dangling for later negotiations. Still, faced with the alternatives of the Vladivostok provisions without coverage of Backfire and cruise missiles or no Vladivostok agreement at all, it would be better to postpone those issues. In that case the committee would almost certainly press for a rapid resumption of talks on those two issues.

6. There is strong sentiment for further exploration of the "qualitative" restrictions of the sort proposed by President Carter in the Moscow packages. We may well be approaching the point where limitations of flight tests themselves are more germane than overall numbers of missiles and launchers, since it is the qualitative improvements, rather than quantitative change, that will pose the greater threat to strategic stability in the years ahead.

Conventional Arms Transfers

Few areas of arms control policy have given us more trouble than conventional arms transfers. Billions of dollars worth of weapons were sold or given away with little consideration of how they would affect the U.S. national interest. Before President Carter announced a new doctrine in May 1977, there had never been a serious administration-backed proposal for control of conventional arms transfers.

The volume of these sales alone demonstrates the increasing significance of the problem. In 1976 an estimated $20 billion worth of conventional arms was sold or, in some cases, given away. And the United States was in the lead, with over half the total sales. As Vice-President Walter Mondale put it, we are no longer the arsenal of democracy, simply the arsenal. Our Foreign Military Sales and Military Assistance grants alone have grown from $1 billion in 1967 to $10 billion in 1975, a figure that dropped a bit in 1976 but will be just as high for

1977. Let me put it another way: since World War II, the United States has sold or given away $125 billion worth of weapons.

Congress has been slow to react to this. Ironically, perhaps the most important single step forward originated with a senator—Gaylord Nelson—who is not a member of the Foreign Relations Committee. Senator Nelson worked long and hard to convince Congress and, in particular, members of the committee that major arms sales should be reviewed and subject to rejection by concurrent resolution. As first passed, the Nelson Amendment provided for a review of proposals over $25 million, with a twenty-day period in which Congress might act. In 1976 the period for review was lengthened to thirty days, and the trigger level lowered to $7 million for major weapon categories.

The viability of the Nelson Amendment procedures was severely challenged in the closing days of the 94th Congress, when the Ford administration proposed a series of arms transfers totaling $6.1 billion, largely to Middle East and Persian Gulf countries. The committee reluctantly acquiesced in these sales, but included with approval a statement that other transfers to this sensitive region would be rejected unless the executive produced an overall policy statement justifying them.

Nevertheless, all of us who lived through this process in committee recognize serious shortcomings in the Nelson procedures:

1. Congress gets into the act only after a sale has been promised by the Pentagon. At this stage Congress can reject a sale only at the risk of creating a serious diplomatic incident. This was the case during the committee's debate on both the Maverick missile sale to Saudi Arabia and the AWACS sales to Iran. It is thus understandable, though not forgivable, that Congress has not passd a single resolution of disapproval since the process of reporting and review was instituted in January 1975.

2. Another nagging problem is whether the required congressional action should be the negative one of vetoing proposed transfers, as is now the case, or the positive step

of approving them. Critics of arms transfers argue that defeating a motion of approval would in many cases be easier than securing a resolution of disapproval.

3. Setting a threshold above which Congress can disapprove sales has proved problematic. Set too high, the threshold can preclude consideration of key weapons. For example, the controversial sale of CBU-72 concussion bombs to Israel was for less than $1 million. Regardless of one's attitude toward the sale, it is obviously the sort of sale the committee should examine but at present does not have the authority to question under the Nelson Amendment.

The difficulties of articulating an overall arms transfer policy, however, were made more apparent in President Carter's May 1977 statement on conventional arms transfer policy. The key policy consideration, as the president explained it, was that in the future, "the burden of persuasion will be on those who favor a particular arms sale, rather than those who oppose it." This, it seems to me, is the proper emphasis.

The president then spelled out six guidelines for transfers: (1) dollar volume for weapons sales in 1978 will be less than in 1977; (2) the U.S. will not be the first supplier to introduce high-level technology into an area; (3) weapons will not be developed solely for export; (4) with some exceptions coproduction agreements will be prohibited; (5) the United States will normally stipulate in advance that it will not entertain any requests for retransfers; and (6) controls on sales agents will be tightened.

The president may achieve his objective of capping total sales, but he faces a series of extremely difficult political and strategic decisions. Blocking Pakistan's purchase of 100 A-17s was not difficult; Pakistan has no Washington lobby. The decision not to sell Iran F-18Ls was sweetened by a concomitant willingness to increase the sale of F-16s. Other impending sales will be ticklish: sophisticated military hardware to Egypt, the beginning of a program for the Sudan, a virtual giveaway to Zaire, and a foot in the door of Somalia.

Praiseworthy as the president's arms transfer policy statement is, such decisions must be based on a broader understanding of overall military, economic, and social factors. Under the law the executive branch is required to prepare arms control impact statements on major weapons programs so Congress can weigh the arms control impact of major programs before voting on either authorization or appropriation.

This requirement makes a lot of sense. For one thing, it should force bureaucrats in the executive branch to weigh more fully the impact of new weapons programs. They have not taken kindly to this idea. The administration fought the legislation until its passage in December 1975, and did not produce the required statements on time. The first series of statements the Foreign Affairs Committee received in 1975 were so poorly prepared that they were rejected as failing to meet the requirements of the law.

Ideally, these statements should probe such questions as:

1. *Political implications.* The long-term prospects for the recipient country's domestic and foreign relations; how it gets along with its neighbors; the sort of government in power and its intentions; the likelihood of trouble in the area; the possibility of the weapon's being misused or transferred to third parties.

2. *Economic impact.* President Carter mentioned in his arms transfer statement the necessity of taking into account the economic impact on the recipient country, particularly one in the developing world, but in practice this is difficult to assess. In most cases nations face a guns or butter choice, and arms purchases inevitably absorb resources that might arguably be better used elsewhere.

3. *Social impact.* If the sale of a weapons system and the training program that accompanies it are successful, they will foster a sophisticated military elite, which will interact with other elements in the society in a political way. One need look no farther than the Middle East for examples of how enormous this impact can be.

4. *Implications for the United States.* How do American companies approach selling weapons abroad? How much of the demand is artificially stimulated by sharp sales practices? What role do our military services play in encouraging sales? To what degree do our Air Force and Army, for instance,

compete for sales?

The central point, it seems to me, is the importance of so-called "back-end" implementation. The United States's involvement with a nation does not stop with an arms sale, but actually balloons with it. Once the contract is signed, we frequently become deeply involved in the affairs of the recipient country—through procurement, finance, logistics, maintenance, and training. It is impossible, for example, to discuss arms sales to Iran without noting that within a few years there will be over 60,000 Americans in Iran servicing weapons we have sold there. It is not irrelevant to recall that this is the number of "technicians" we had in Vietnam in mid 1965.

Nuclear Proliferation

The third category I wish to develop is nuclear proliferation. It is apparent that the Carter administration has launched an all-out effort to achieve restraints on reactor technology and fuel reprocessing. The dimensions of this problem are enormous. More than thirty nations have built or have under construction some 300 nuclear power reactors, and a major by-product of nuclear fission in a power reactor is spent fuel rods containing plutonium, from which bombs can be made.

Congress has tried to come to grips with this problem. The 94th Congress passed the Symington Amendment to the International Security Assistance and Arms Export Control Act of 1976, which required a cut-off of all military and most economic assistance to nations selling or buying enrichment or reprocessing equipment, materials, or technology—unless the nations involved in the transfer agreed to put the enrichment and reprocessing equipment under multilateral auspices and management, and then agreed to full international safeguards in all nuclear programs.

Despite opposition from the Ford administration, the amendment was approved. Ironically, then Secretary of State Kissinger immediately embraced it in trying to dissuade Pakistan from buying a nuclear reprocessing plant from France. The amendment also figured in similar discussions aimed at persuading Brazil and West Germany to drop plans for a fuel-reprocessing system in their billion-dollar nuclear deal.

In 1977 Congress approved tougher legislation in the Glenn Amendment to the International Security Assistance and Arms Export Control Act of 1977. The Glenn Amendment provides for the same military and economic cut-offs as the Symington Amendment, with one important difference: the two conditions under which transfers could be approved are eliminated, and the transfer of reprocessing equipment, material, or technology between individual nations automatically triggers a cut-off.

Conclusion

A review of all these programs facing the Foreign Relations Committee, together with the determination repeatedly expressed by the executive to proceed with SALT, arms sale limitations, and antiproliferation efforts, leads inescapably to the conclusion that we face an era in which the Foreign Relations Committee will be heavily engaged across the spectrum of arms control. Of course, predicting congressional behavior is always risky. The rather ragged performance of the committee at times in the past underscores the danger of predicting too far in the future. Optimism can quickly turn to pessimism.

But the record in recent years shows a steady improvement. To be sure, too often the committee and the Congress have left the initiative in arms control to the executive. Increasingly, however, Congress, too, has made a contribution. The Jackson Amendment regarding SALT I, requiring that we maintain equal aggregates, has become a guideline for SALT II. Another example was the refusal to fund a second ABM site, which led to the official retrenchment to one site in 1974. But there are other reasons for predicting confidently a new and enhanced role for the Foreign Relations Committee.

There is, first of all, the clear-cut determination of President Carter himself to accord arms control issues top priority. He has also come to recognize the necessity of closer cooperation with Congress on these issues. An adversary relationship is an impediment to effective administration. I would now expect a more constructive approach to some of the legislative ideas that have been presented regarding arms control.

But the basic reason for my conviction that the Foreign Relations Committee will be more active is that arms control issues are forcing themselves upon us; decisions on arms limitations, on arms transfers, on proliferation, simply have to be taken. They are no longer issues we can take up at our convenience. As an observer noted at the Paul Warnke confirmation hearing, the long lines outside the hearing room testify to the public sense of urgency. This urgency is fully shared by members of the Foreign Relations Committee.

6
The Control of United States Arms Sales

Philip J. Farley

Congress is neither an outsider nor powerless with regard to the sale of arms by the United States. The authority of the executive branch to sell arms to other countries, as well as its authority to regulate commercial exports, derives from legislation. Legislation prescribes the objectives, general criteria, and many specific guidelines for arms sales. Increasing masses of information on prospective or completed sales flow to congressional committees in regular reports or in testimony at hearings. In 1974 the president was required by law to submit any proposed governmental foreign military sales (FMS) of more than $25 million to Congress, which then had twenty days in which to block the sale by concurrent resolution. After one presidential veto, a comprehensive Arms Export Control Act, consolidating and expanding legislative guidance and oversight, was passed in 1976 at the initiative of Congress.

Despite passage of this new legislation, congressional impact on the U.S. role in the world arms trade remains uncertain. Our sales of defense articles and services continue to be high; while FMS orders for Fiscal Year 1976 totaled an estimated $8.7 billion in comparison with the peak of $10.6 billion in Fiscal 1974, the decline is attributable to saturation of the Middle East and Persian Gulf markets, rather than to American restraint fostered by Congress. Not one congressional resolution blocking a prospective sale has been passed. Reflecting the uncertainty about achievements and prospects, the 1976 Arms Export Control Act requested two basic studies: a presidential study of arms sales policies and practices, and a comprehensive report by the secretary of state on the effects of the act's provisions on U.S. policy, both to be submitted to the Congress by June 30, 1977. Arms sales, the policies governing them, and the role of Congress in influencing them remained controversial issues as the Carter administration began.

Arms Transfers and Arms Sales

A few explanatory points will help clarify the data and legislative language used in the following.

Arms sales are made both by the government as FMS and by private firms under government license. The great bulk of sales are FMS: over $10 billion in Fiscal 1975, as against less than $600 million in commercial exports. The commercial share is unlikely to increase; the 1976 act required any sale to non-NATO countries of $25 million or more to be handled through FMS channels.

The term "sales" relates to orders or agreements to purchase; these are the most familiar and best publicized FMS figures. Actual deliveries or exports lag considerably. While FMS sales in Fiscal 1976 totaled nearly $8.7 billion worldwide, deliveries were $4 billion. At the end of Fiscal 1976 the backlog of undelivered orders was nearly $32 billion, with delivery schedules extending up to 1982. As a result annual delivery rates obviously will rise. Data on commercial transactions are available only for deliveries, but since they increasingly do not include major military equipment with long production and delivery schedules, there is not a comparable backlog.

While the terms arms sales and arms transfers will be used, they embrace more than lethal hardware. The more precise term is "defense articles and services." Executive branch estimates are that 60 percent of the value of FMS pertain to services, support equipment, and spare parts, and 40 percent to major military equipment and other arms and ammunition. "Services" includes not only training, maintenance, and technical advice, but also major construction projects: of nearly $2.5 billion in FMS to Saudi Arabia in Fiscal 1976, $2 billion was for construction projects. Another noteworthy component is sales of equipment and technology for foreign production of weapons.

All arms transfers by the United States are not sales, governmental or commercial. There is still a Military Assistance Program (MAP), though it is dwindling. MAP deliveries and expenditures totaled nearly $5 billion as recently as Fiscal 1973, falling to about $2 billion for Fiscal 1975 and $300 million for Fiscal 1976. (For comparison, total FMS and commercial deliveries for these years were $1.7, $4, and about $4.7 billion respectively.)

The current overall arms transfer level of $5 to 6 billion annually which results from combining these aid and trade figures is not greatly different (in current dollars, without allowance for inflation) from levels prevailing in the 1960s, though then the larger share by far was aid. And twenty-five years ago, in Fiscal 1952, annual military assistance appropriations peaked at $5.7 billion in 1952 dollars—almost exactly the present annual value of American arms transfers in inflated current dollars.

Not only has the predominant form of transfer changed from aid to sales, so has the principal destination. Europe was the primary recipient area in the 1950s, Southeast Asia in the 1960s, and the Persian Gulf and Middle East in the 1970s (of the over $35 billion in FMS for 1973-76, over $23 billion, or nearly two-thirds, went to just three counties—Iran, Saudi Arabia, and Israel).

The security assistance program includes an FMS credit program. Funds appropriated for this purpose are used either to finance purchases or, predominantly, to guarantee private loans for arms purchases by countries in which the U.S. has a security interest. Through Fiscal 1976 the FMS credit program totaled somewhat over $10 billion, out of total postwar FMS of nearly $47 billion—slightly over 20 percent. Credits are justified as promoting security and political purposes, not sales. Since most sales are made without official credit assistance, the United States obviously does not need to offer easy credit to compete in the world arms market. The sales financed by FMS credits are included in the overall sales and delivery figures given earlier.

MAP and other security assistance programs have always been subject to congressional control because they are dependent on the annual appropriation and authorization of funds. In recent years Congress has scrutinized them with increasing care and has applied tighter and more detailed constraints. The 1976 act provides for phasing out MAP except for countries and amounts that would be specifically authorized later. For arms sales, only transactions using FMS credits have been subject to this prior review and authorization, and even this review had often been quite general.

Legislation

Until the act of 1976, government regulation and licensing of commercial sales rested on a single sentence in Section 414 of the Mutual Security Act of 1954: "The President is authorized to control, in futherance of world peace and the security and foreign policy of the United States, the export and import of arms, ammunition, and implements of war, including technical data relating thereto." The licensing program has been administered by the Office of Munitions Control in the Bureau of Political-Military Affairs of the Department of State. Detailed implementing regulations have been promulgated by the president without congressional review. Congress has given relatively little attention to commercial sales. A requirement that all licenses issued be reported to Congress was not appended to the governing legislation until 1973, though some reports on export volume had been submitted before this. The government's FMS activities initially found their authorization in the Mutual Security Act and its successor, the Foreign Assistance Act of 1961. While sales were by no means insignificant (a total of $13.5 billion through Fiscal 1968, with annual levels around $1 billion in the mid 1960s), they were small in comparison to military assistance. They were also viewed rather benevolently in the Congress. Sales were considered the preferred mode for transferring arms that enabled other countries to defend themselves, with MAP a temporary stop-gap burden on the American taxpayer; Section 505(c) of the Foreign Assistance Act provided that grant aid should be deliberately reduced and then terminated as recipients acquired sufficient wealth to support their own military needs.

In the late 1960s, however, rising government sales attracted more skeptical congressional attention. An adverse balance of payments, due in part to the United States's overseas military expenditures, led to aggressive and at times conspicuous Defense Department efforts to sell arms in West Germany, Japan, Iran, and other dollar-rich, friendly countries. The department used revenues from FMS as a revolving fund for future credits. Other arms sales were financed by the Export-Import Bank under what was known as the "Country X" arrangement: the Bank was not informed who the purchasing country was, but simply accepted Defense Department certification of the proposed transaction. Although this clandestine-sounding arrangement was made at the behest of the Bank, which thought thereby to insulate itself from military and political entanglements, it had a devious and ominous appearance. Like the revolving fund, it also looked like an effort to evade congressional oversight. After hearings before the Senate Foreign Relations Committee, these practices were terminated. The executive branch submitted draft legislation to separate FMS from security assistance, and to put the FMS credit program on an open and regular basis.

The Foreign Military Sales Act was passed in 1968 in much the same form as the executive had submitted it. It governed FMS in the early 1970s, and its structure and basic provisions survive in the Arms Export Control Act of 1976, which superseded it.

Arms Sales Policy as Expressed in Legislation

It is possible to regard arms sales as intrinsically bad or dangerous or politically undesirable, to be avoided except perhaps to close allies. With various nuances this is the stay-out-of-trouble approach of Japan, West Germany, and Sweden. It is also possible to view arms sales as just another form of international trade, to be promoted for the sake of favorable trade balance and to support domestic arms industries and employment; this approach prevails in France and Britain.

American policy views arms sales as inherently neither good nor bad. The opening sections of the Foreign Military Sales Act, now the Arms Export Control Act, set forth "foreign and national security policy objectives and restraints." The ultimate U.S. goal, the act declares, is a world free of war and the dangers and burdens of armaments. In the meantime, defense and armaments may be necessary, and producing their own arms may not be economical for many countries. To be approved, FMS must be consistent with U.S. foreign policy interests and with the military, economic, and financial situations of purchasing countries. Applicable criteria and procedures include the following:

1. Sales should meet such valid defense needs of "friendly countries" as internal security; legitimate self-defense; participation in United Nations or other collective peace-keeping measures; and civic action (e.g., road building, medical, and similar peacetime activities) undertaken by the armed forces. FMS shall be made "solely" to achieve one or more of these purposes (Section 4).

2. In addition, the president must find that the sale will strengthen U.S. security and promote world peace (Section 3). This test looks beyond the defense interest of the purchaser to ask what are the *United States* and *world* interests. (Thus President Ford, when questioned on January 27, 1975, about his administration's supplying of arms to both sides in the Middle East, responded that the purpose was to help recipients maintain internal security and to maintain a military equilibrium in the region, thus facilitating negotiations and diplomatic efforts.) Similar broad considerations, it will be recalled, are cited in Section 414 of the Mutual Security Act, the basis for regulation of commercial sales.

3. Several concerns about the possible consequences of arms sales are reflected in the act. Section 42 specifically requires that, before approval, the executive must consider whether a sale might contribute to an arms race; increase the possibility of an outbreak or escalation of conflict; prejudice development of bilateral or multilateral arms control arrangements; or—in

cases involving government credit or guarantee for arrangements licensing production or coproduction abroad—have adverse effects on production and employment within the United States (economic or commercial advantages are *not* listed as a consideration in the Foreign Military Sales Act or the Arms Export Control Act).

4. Sales should not be approved, except on waiver by the president, "where they would have the effect of arming military dictators who are denying the growth of fundamental rights or social progress to their own people" (Section 1). Military (and also economic) assistance is to be denied governments that intern or imprison their citizens for political purposes.

5. Several other provisions are designed to identify and forestall undesirable consequences:

- arms must not be retransferred to a country other than the original purchaser without United States consent;
- arms must be used for the purposes for which the United States furnishes them;
- arms and related technology must be given security protection by the recipient;
- sales to countries that seize American fishing vessels shall be suspended; and
- purchase of excessive or sophisticated military equipment must not compete with economic development or occasion diversion of economic aid. (The first four provisions are from Section 3, the last from Sections 4 and 35.)

To make these provisions enforceable, the standard FMS contract contains a clause (Section A.6) reserving the right of the United States to cancel all or any part of an order before delivery of goods or services, provided it pay all termination costs. The Arms Export Control Act requires, in Section 42 (c), that such a cancellation provision be included in every sales contract or license. Countries violating such provisions may also become ineligible for future purchases.

6. Sales can only be made to countries "otherwise eligible" (Section 3). Among others, this excludes Communist countries

and those under Soviet "domination" (Mutual Defense Assistance Control Act of 1951—the Battle Act).

In addition to explicit legislative criteria for arms sales, the executive branch routinely applies several other tests, which should be noted to round out the picture:

1. Sales must not contravene international measures that we support (e. g., the United Nations embargoes directed against South Africa or Rhodesia).
2. Sales must not be made that violate our obligations under international agreements (thus some sales of computers and guidance systems have been barred as inconsistent with provisions of the Limited Test Ban Treaty and the Non-Proliferation Treaty.
3. Current U.S. foreign policy restrictions will be applied (thus for a number of years an embargo on shipment of lethal end-items was applied to India and Pakistan).
4. Particularly since the 1973 Arab-Israeli hostilities and the heavy drawdown of U.S. stocks in the course of resupplying Israel, explicit consideration has been given to the impact of a proposed sale on the readiness of United States forces. The Arms Export Control Act incorporated this criterion by requiring in Section 21 (h) presidential justification of any sale with a significant adverse impact.
5. There is a presumption against supplying certain sensitive weapons, such as hand-transportable surface-to-air missiles (especially dangerous if falling into terrorist hands), or weapons primarily for use against crowds.
6. Particularly in the case of allied developing countries, the United States military advisory group in the country must judge that the purchaser will be able to handle and maintain the equipment sold.

In the controversy over arms sales and pertinent legislation, which culminated in the Arms Export Control Act of 1976, no new issues or ideas were raised. There was an uneasy sense in Congress that too many arms were being sold, by the United

States and by other countries; there was skepticism that arms sales could be counted on to advance international security or American influence; there was doubt that proper weight was being given, in arms sales efforts and decisions, to arms control possibilities or to the position of purchasing governments on human rights, discrimination, or international terrorism. There was also a recognition that individual decisions are difficult, and that general changes in policies and programs capable of effecting a transformation in the arms trade have still to be devised.

Thus the thrust of the 1976 legislation is toward encouraging a more careful weighing of the pros and cons before the executive branch promotes a sale, providing more, and less restricted, information to enhance congressional and public knowledge and influence, and affording Congress the authority and opportunity to reach different conclusions on major cases when its sense of foreign policy interests or the consequences of an arms sale diverges from that of the executive. (This last, formal congressional involvement in program decisions was initiated by the Nelson Amendment of 1974, to be discussed later.) The Arms Control Act of 1976 has the following provisions:

1. The structure and most of the substance of the Foreign Military Sales Act are retained.

2. Regulation and licensing of commercial exports of defense articles and services are embraced in this act, and the relevent Section 414 of the Mutual Security Act is repealed. Except for NATO countries, no commercial license for export of major defense equipment may exceed $25 million; large sales are to be handled on a government-to-government basis and subject to congressional review and veto.

3. The period within which Congress can block by concurrent resolution an arms sale of $25 million or more is extended to thirty calendar days. The procedure also applies to sales of major defense equipment valued at $7 million or more, in cases where Congress finds that violation of human rights or discrimination against American personnel requires termination, and where there has been substantial violations by a country of the terms of earlier sales agreements.

4. The information to be furnished by the executive on sales and export licenses is specified in considerable detail, to be unclassified unless this would be "clearly detrimental" to U.S. security.

5. The act's policy statement encouraging the limitation of arms transfers is strengthened. The director of the Arms Control and Disarmament Agency is to be consulted regarding export licenses. Notifications to Congress of prospective major sales or licenses are to include an analysis of the arms control impact. In the president's comprehensive study of the U.S. arms sales policies and practices, he is to give particular attention to possible approaches to limiting the arms trade.

6. The policy of promoting respect for human rights and freedoms is restated, as is the policy that no security assistance (including sales or licenses for export of defense articles and services) be provided to countries engaged in consistent gross violations of human rights. A Coordinator for Human Rights is established in the Department of State to provide relevant information, and an explanation is required of any extraordinary circumstances that may necessitate continuation of assistance in the face of human rights violations.

7. Sales and licenses are prohibited in the case of countries engaging in discrimination against any American citizen, and American agencies are barred from acceding to discrimination; the president may waive this provision on national interest grounds, subject to congressional override by concurrent resolution.

8. Provisions specifying ineligibility for further deliveries or sales in cases of violations of sales agreements are restated and strengthened.

9. Presidential justification and certification is required for any sale adversely affecting U.S. combat readiness.

10. Specific restrictions are stipulated (e. g., sales to Turkey or Chile are prohibited).

11. Reports are required regarding fees, political contributions, and gifts associated with government and commercial sales, and reimbursement of such costs under procurement contracts is regulated.

12. Economic objectives for arms sales abroad continue to go

unmentioned. The president's comprehensive study of arms sales is to take into account "the benefits to the U.S. of such arms sales," but economic impact is specifically mentioned— and then in a negative sense—only with reference to the impact on developing countries.

13. As first passed, the act imposed a ceiling of $9 billion on sales agreements. President Ford's veto message objected to this as arbitrary, as obstructing American industry in competing for orders, and as limiting U.S. ability to meet its friends' legitimate defense needs. The final text dropped the ceiling, but the accompanying congressional report expresses the sense of the conferees that "U.S. arms sales should not exceed current levels" and invites the president to report his findings on the issue of a future ceiling.

Giving Congress Clout

The Arms Control Act of 1976, then, is the culmination of a clearly marked phase in arms sales legislation. Further legislative action is of course possible; some proposals will be examined later. But the act of 1976 completes the shifting of emphasis from pursuit and even promotion of arms sales to their control and regulation. Policy and procedures relating to commercial and government arms sales are brought under the same legislative framework. Reporting and publication of sales data are emphasized in the interests both of congressional knowledge and oversight and of public understanding. The act highlights countervailing national interests—arms control, human rights, priority to equipping U.S. defense forces—to be weighed in arms export decisions.

Passing legislation is one thing; affecting individual or aggregate arms sales is another. Judged by the latter test, legislative prescriptions have had a dubious effect. Overall FMS levels are declining somewhat, from a peak of $10.6 billion in new sales agreements in Fiscal 1974, to $8.7 billion for Fiscal 1976, an estimated $8.8 billion in Fiscal 1977, and a projected $7.7 billion for Fiscal 1978. The decline—somewhat more substantial because of inflation than these constant-dollar figures suggest—is attributed by few observers, in or out of Congress, to congressional influence. Heavy buying from Israel and the Persian Gulf countries, and the $2 billion NATO advanced fighter contract, produced temporarily high levels in the early 1970s from which some drop was predictable. Many individual sales or country sales levels continue to excite criticism and controversy—because they are to dictators, or to one or both participants in actual or potential conflict, or to countries where economic development seems more urgent than military procurement. Congressional mandates appear to be flouted.

As is so often the case, general legislative principles are not self-applying. Judgment is required in each instance, and differing interests or assessments lead to differing conclusions. Different criteria may point in opposite directions in a particular case: South Korea and Ethiopia seek arms for obvious internal and external security reasons, but both are authoritarian and repressive, and Ethiopia is now Marxist and anti-American as well as poverty-stricken. And Turkey, while a NATO ally, has made little movement toward a Cyprus settlement. Should arms be sold or withheld? What are "valid" defense requirements? Acquisition of advanced equipment in the Persian Gulf or Latin America will be assessed by some not as a legitimate response to national danger but as another step in a regional arms race; others will see military build-ups as strengthening self-defense and creating stabilizing military balances, and the United States as a less disruptive supplier than other ready sellers. What some regard as an intolerable degree of domestic repression by an autocratic regime, others see as regrettable but not sufficient cause to bar arms sales that would knit politically desirable alignments or maintain a regional power balance.

Thus, if Congress is interested not only in the rules but also in how the game is actually played, it must go beyond legislative principles. Two ways of doing so have emerged.

One is to pass unqualified specific proscriptions. The Arms Export Control Act of 1976 bars all arms sales to Chile. This is effective, but Congress will not often find a majority for so clear-cut a measure. Being aware of how suddenly events can change, how complex situations can be, and how ruling ourselves out of a changing situation can prevent the United States from influencing developments, Congress is understandably reluctant to pass such sweeping edicts. General proscriptions, on the other hand, as on furnishing arms to regimes that systematically violate human rights, almost always provide for exceptions if the president determines that there are overriding security or national interest considerations.

But what if the exceptions appear to become the rule—if sales seem never to be withheld on grounds of human rights violations or higher priority needs for economic development? And broader still, what if the cumulative effect of sales to a country or region is to establish a relationship between the United States and other countries that carries with it commitments or involvement or positions that Congress does not support? Senator Gaylord Nelson put it this way on June 6, 1974:

> These foreign military sales constitute major foreign policy decisions involving the United States in military activities without sufficient deliberation. This has gotten us into trouble in the past and could easily do so again. . . . Perhaps these transactions—in the Persian Gulf, in Latin America, anywhere—have merit. Perhaps they do not. Without debating the merits of these sales, it seems to me that they represent such a qualitative change in our involvement in the Persian Gulf area and such a significant turn in our Latin American relations, that Congress must be afforded an opportunity to deliberate on these matters.

He therefore introduced the Nelson Amendment, passed in December 1974 as Section 36(b) of the Foreign Military Sales Act, requiring the president to submit in advance to Congress information on any proposed sale of $25 million or more; Congress would have the power to block the sale by concurrent resolution within twenty calendar days unless the sale were certified by the president as a national security emergency.

The Arms Export Control Act of 1976 extends this reverse veto approach to other classes of arms sales and the period for congressional action to thirty days. One argument President

Ford gave for vetoing the act (his veto was not upheld) was that the reverse veto impinged on the president's constitutional responsibility for the conduct of foreign relations. That objection was weak, given the existence of numerous precedents, including the 1974 Nelson Amendment and the provision in the Atomic Energy Act from 1958 on for rejection by current resolution of proposed nuclear cooperation agreements with other nations.

Legal precedents aside, is it improper for Congress to reserve authority to block individual sales? Congress's role lies in the formulation of foreign policy, not its execution. But foreign policy is built upon individual and cumulative decisions, actions, and positions, as well as declarations. Foreign policy on human rights is not just what we say, but what we do. If arms furnished for NATO defense are used to invade Cyprus, U.S. policy on furnishing arms for agreed purposes will be tested by whether further deliveries to Turkey are suspended— as they were not by the executive branch, until Congress imposed a suspension. And such episodes have policy implications: we cannot expect Arab countries to refrain from transshipping American arms to combatant nations in the next Middle East conflict if they have observed others ignoring such contractual commitments with impunity. Arms sales, their political weight in shaping foreign relations, and the associated American presence in other countries—these are major elements in foreign policy, and if Congress is indeed to be an equal partner in shaping foreign policy to correspond to the national will and national interest, it cannot confine itself to general declarations. Nor can oversight be effective if limited to admonitions. The reverse veto enables Congress to express its will if a substantial majority reaches a conclusion different from the executive's on matters where it shares responsibility.

Ironically, given the controversy over the reverse veto, it has never been formally employed. No blocking concurrent resolution has ever been passed.

Does Congress Have an Impact?

Despite the continuing high levels of sales and the absence

of blocking concurrent resolutions, it would be wrong to conclude that Congress lacks influence on arms sales or that a clear congressional mandate is being frustrated by the executive branch and arms manufacturers.

In the first place, one cannot assume that the critics of arms sales speak for Congress. Congressional sentiment is probably best summed up by Senator Hubert Humphrey, whose subcommittee of the Senate Foreign Relations Committee took the lead in putting together the 1976 act. His position was that arms sales are neither good nor bad *a priori;* they require a careful balancing of pros and cons by the executive branch in each case, oversight by Congress, and much greater openness to public and congressional scrutiny. So long as the executive appears to have conscientiously considered the risks and consequences of a sale, a majority of congressmen will give great weight to the executive's conclusion that a sale is warranted. If a sale has no obviously detrimental security, political, or arms control impact, most congressmen will see no reason why the United States should forego a sale for abstract, indirect reasons. Public opinion on arms sales is diffuse and unfocused, and Congress reflects this faithfully. There is a general repugnance toward massive arms sales and uneasiness about American preeminence in the trade. But there is also responsiveness to the argument that if sales are going to be made by someone, it might as well be the United States (and thus be American firms and workers who get the orders), assuming there are no concrete reasons against the sale (such as the repressiveness of the Chilean or South Korean governments, or ethnic groups' opposition to arms sales to Arab nations or Turkey). The human rights, arms control, and political ramifications of arms sales reflected in the 1976 act are acknowledged by most members of Congress, but invoking them to bar a sale to a nonhostile country requires specific demonstration that they apply, and that they are not outweighed by security and political advantages.

Congress is not subservient to commercial or labor representations in this area. When a sale is being questioned, interested manufacturers, local groups, labor representatives, and the congressional representatives are heard. But their arguments will not override weighty security, political, or arms control objections. Armaments manufacturers did lobby against the Arms Export Control Act of 1976. Their clumsy, transparently narrow efforts, however, reflected in a self-serving memorandum that was circulated in Congress and fell into the hands of the bill's supporters, were counterproductive. They probably helped assure passage of the bill by under-cutting more substantive executive branch objections to the political inflexibility and adminstrative inefficiency imposed by the act.

Congress, in sum, is not more hostile to arms sales than the executive. It is more responsive to a diverse constituency and is itself more diverse, and thus disposed to see more than one side of an argument and to give opponents a day in court. Sometimes this leads to pressure for sales, as in the case of Israel. If Congress passed on all arms sales, it is far from certain that the outcome would differ greatly from that of the executive branch, or that the annual sales volumes would be lower.

In regard to particular sales, Congress's influence is not adequately measured by the absence of blocking resolutions. The threat of an adverse vote has enabled interested members to influence administration plans and decisions. Congressional suspicion that accepting sale of C-130 airplanes to Egypt might be followed by sales of more sophisticated weapons systems led to an understanding that, in return for not blocking that sale, it would not be followed immediately by proposals for additional military sales. The idea of Pershing missiles for Israel was dropped following congressional criticism and representa-tions. The number of Hawks and Sidewinders sold to Saudi Arabia was cut back in response to congressional objections.

The more pervasive impact of the reverse veto power is on the vigor and quality of the executive's review of arms sales proposals. Known congressional views on the importance of human rights, arms control, or priority of American forces' needs, and the prospect that an arms sale might be questioned on these grounds, give proponents of these interests within the executive agencies an opening and a right they would otherwise not have. Since the great preponderance of attention to the consequences of a sale occurs within the executive branch, strengthening the adversary aspect of the review process there is important and a significant multiplier of congressional influence. Simply passing hortatory legislation is unlikely to have a comparable effect; it is the prospect of protracted hearings or opposition before a sale can be consummated that induces careful executive scrutiny of proposed sales. And inducing critical review at the precommitment stage is doubly advantageous in that it is easier to say no than simply to defer a decision; once an agreement, however conditional, has been reached between the executive and another country, it becomes much more difficult for Congress to impose a veto, and much more costly politically if it does so.

The basic concern of Congress is with policy, as expressed in the first instance in legislation, and then in assessing executive performance through reports and hearings. In this oversight function Congress must at times play an adversary role. Having no direct responsibility for arms sales, Congress is often more objective in assessing sales in which the executive may have a proprietary interest or emotional commitment. In recent years presidents and their principal advisers have been disposed to see arms purchases by nonhostile states as regionally stabilizing rather than threatening or competitive; arms sales by the United States have been considered productive of useful political influence rather than politically risky. Congress has been more disposed to be wary, to look to future uncertainties or awkward consequences as well as immediate diplomatic gains. And since the consequences of arms sales can be ambiguous and debatable, and political situations and alignments in purchasing nations may change while the arms, once delivered, remain under a regime's control, the value of skeptical scrutiny is clear. Even when it is motivated by partisan, doctrinaire, or ethnic loyalties, the result can be a constructive change.

One consequence may be change or refinement of legislation. There may be pressure on the executive to alter the way it administers programs. Or there may be changes in executive attitudes and priorities, as has appeared to be happening early in the Carter administration. New national leaders, of course, have their own ideas and policies. But the outspoken views and persistent actions of congressional critics of past arms sales have surely shaped public perceptions and receptiveness to reform, in addition to preparing segments of the bureaucracy to respond to new directions.

Further Legislation and the Future Role of Congress

The thrust of the Arms Export Control Act of 1976 is toward restraint and balance in administrative procedures and guidelines, in aggregate levels of arms sales approved, and in identifying the direction to be taken in influencing the scope and character of the world arms trade—a trade in which the United States plays the largest single part.

Congress will undoubtedly insist on continued accountability and pursue its oversight function vigorously. Specific sales or issues will occasion debate and controversy and bargaining—arms sales to Greece and Turkey, levels and types of arms for Israel, sales to Arab states. Required policy studies pursuant to the 1976 act and presidential policy statements will occasion questioning and assessment, followed by expressions of support or dissatisfaction, or countersuggestions.

If in the first year of the Carter administration it is generally concluded that arms sales are being handled reflectively and wisely, recent suspicions and the disposition to assert congressional prerogatives may diminish. Difficult and controversial cases will always arise from time to time, and be argued and fought over. Otherwise, the executive may be expected to administer arms sales in an atmosphere of greater mutual confidence. The reverse veto would remain on the books, but recourse to it would be rarely considered.

Accord and consensus, however, may prove more elusive than this suggests. As the new administration establishes its own links with the seventy or so countries purchasing arms under the FMS program, discovers the political as well as security weight they attach to access to American supplies, and realizes the difficulty of rejecting clients or of affecting purchasers' demands or other suppliers' attitudes, the U.S. role in the arms market may appear unchanged except in the accompanying rhetoric. Calls for new legislation or other congressional action would then arise once more. How may Congress try to affect the general level or direction of arms sales? Some past proposals of doubtful value may resurface:

1. *Congressional approval of each major sale.* This would in effect make Congress the executive, and leave executive agencies with merely a routine administrative role. Congressional decision making on this scale is impractical. The executive branch exists precisely for this purpose. Congress is too cumbersome, too heterogeneous, too busy with other pressing matters, and, moreover, is unlikely to do any better. If executive decisions proved consistently objectionable to a majority in Congress, the reasonable remedy would be broad legislation aimed at the policies or programs underlying the objectionable decisions.

2. *Ceilings, global or regional.* Ceilings can be useful, as they have proved when applied in the past to South Korea, Turkey, Latin America, and Africa. They have, however, an arbitrary character. The proper principle—implicit in the legislation of 1976—is that no sale should be made, even within a ceiling, unless sound; and that any sale warranted on security and political grounds should be approved whether or not it exceeds the ceiling. Ceilings are therefore at best temporary ways of resolving sharp differences—as in the cases of South Korea and Turkey—or of expressing a hope that sales can be held down—as in the cases of Latin America and Africa, where ceilings were promptly abandoned once they became constraining.

3. *Advance approval of sales to particular nations or regions.* This approach raises awkward administrative problems, since sales are not programmed in the same way as foreign assistance programs or appropriations. Its effect is as likely to be toward padding programs as toward thinning them down. The present practice of submitting general forecasts annually should suffice to alert Congress to situations that may warrant investigation.

Congress might more fruitfully explore the following approaches:

1. *Annual hearings on regional arms projections.* Those who call for closer attention to arms sales claim that they

influence or even make foreign policy and foreign commitments, and affect regional peace and stability. Yet sales tend to
be looked at piecemeal or *ad hoc,* outside their proper context
and stripped of their real-life complexity of motivation and
consequences. A rare exception was the inquiry in 1974 and
1975, by a subcommittee of the House Committee on
International Relations, into arms sales to the Persian Gulf.
For the major arms-purchasing areas it would not be excessive
for appropriate committees to have such hearings annually or
biennially. Sales could then be put into proper perspective in
relation to regional situations and trends; U.S. policy toward
the region and toward individual states; alternative political,
military, and economic means of pursuing our goals; the
consequences of continuing arms sales or of restricting them;
avenues for limitation that the United States might pursue
unilaterally or in cooperation with other suppliers of the states
in a given region. All these factors are related: they constitute
the context in which the wisdom of an arms sale can best be
judged, and possible changes in programs or legislation best
assessed. At present, debate tends to focus on individual cases,
and general considerations may be used to win the argument
rather than to illuminate the problem. Better policy and better
decisions are more likely to result from a more regular and
deliberate consultative process.

   2. *Opening up the arms sales process.* Continued congressional pressure is needed to keep information flowing on arms
sales and related commitments. The situation has changed
radically for the better in recent years, but providing data in a
timely and intelligible fashion is burdensome for the
bureaucracy and in many cases distasteful to other countries
and to American firms. Congress can insist it be given not only
the facts on what is being sold to whom, but meaningful
explanations of the reasons and risks. In requiring "arms
control impact statements" to accompany notices of major
pending arms sales, Congress was asking for such explanations, but the initial impact statements have been weak. In
some instances, of course, arms control considerations may be
peripheral and some broader form of justification preferable.
However done—in connection with particular sales or in

annual program forecasts and hearings—the facts and implications should be unearthed and understood. Some cases with delicate political implications may warrant secrecy, as may some commercial and technical details. In general, however, access to information serves the public interests, and this is particularly true of a field so directly related to international relations and commitments. The flow of information will inevitably dwindle in the absence of congressional insistence.

3. *Policy changes and reinforcements.* What is needed now is not more policy pronouncements, but a more restrained and objective application of existing legislative and executive doctrine. Possibilities that merit consideration include:

- Tighter controls on exports of some categories of weapons, such as weapons specially adapted to offensive warfare, advanced or sophisticated weapons, types not previously deployed in a region, police weapons usuable against crowds or popular movements in authoritarian states, weapons seen as indiscriminate or cruel (napalm, concussion bombs, etc.)
- Tighter controls on transfer of technology or equipment for local arms production to slow proliferation of conventional arms capabilities and of arms suppliers. (The sale of arms, however, may help or force a country into local arms production, thereby making it self-reliant.)
- Careful screening of FMS credits to make sure they serve the security and political interests of both the United States and the recipient, rather than simply bolstering sales.
- Possibly developing economic adjustment mechanisms, should arms sales fall off or are limited by unilateral or multilateral measures, so that the impact of reduced sales does not fall unfairly on particular regions or groups of workers.

Policy adjustments of this kind might be made by the executive within existing legislation. Some such measures were announced by the Carter administration in early 1977.

However, amendments to the Arms Export Control Act might reinforce executive policy, or stimulate executive action or public understanding of the reasons for it. In any case congressional oversight and at times action on arms transfers will continue to be important. Whether dealing with military assistance or arms sales, Congress has at its disposal one of its most effective levers for guiding our relations with other countries.

Conclusion

It is unlikely that the United States will soon relinquish its preeminence in the world arms trade. Nor would such a change turn the world toward peace and stability. Indeed, it is constructive political and security measures by the United States—designed to avoid conflict, reduce tensions, alleviate the poverty and injustice that underlie much disorder and instability, and generally to reinforce the bases of peace—that will lead to diminished reliance on military power and thus to reduced demand for arms.

In the present world, arms are tragically often an actual or perceived condition of peace and security—but not all arms, and not everywhere. It is too easy to justify an arms sale as stabilizing or as yielding us valuable political influence. And it is too easy to override doubts on these scores with the rationale that "If we don't sell, another (perhaps less benign) country will," without actually attempting to prevent that from happening through cooperation with purchasers or other sellers.

Judgment, restraint, openness to new approaches—all these are more important in managing and constraining arms sales than are dramatic changes in policy. The decisive role will thus inevitably be played by the executive branch. That is its function, which Congress cannot assume. What Congress can do is to lay down sound and balanced policy, exhort and encourage and criticize, object to questionable decisions or trends and on occasion take action to block them, and make sure that the press and the people know what is being done, so that interest groups or opinion at large can express dissatisfaction. In recent years Congress has done a better job than the executive branch in seeing that arms sales accord with the national interest. If the executive has been moving toward a more discriminating and moderate position, much of the credit goes to Congress. Congressional oversight, debate, and constructive criticism will continue to be essential in holding arms sales to their proper subordinate places in the foreign policy of the United States.

7
Congress and Nonproliferation, 1945-1977

Warren H. Donnelly

The proliferation of nuclear weapons and the capacity to make them is regarded by many members of Congress as a principal danger of the nuclear era. Since the end of World War II, both the executive and legislative branches of the United States government have helped devise and carry out policies designed to prevent proliferation. This shared interest has helped maintain that tension between the two branches of the government considered desirable under our Constitution.

The role of Congress in nonproliferation policy illustrates its potential role in the broader area of arms control. Since Congress has just entered what may be a period of sustained attention to nonproliferation, it is pertinent to examine briefly what is role has been, where it has run ahead of the executive, and where it has been quiescent.

Congressional Attitude toward Proliferation

The proliferation of nuclear weapons among other countries, and perhaps even criminal or dissident groups within nations, is considered by many congressmen a leading, perhaps *the* leading, danger of our times. To date congressional

The views expressed are solely those of the author and should not be considered views of the Congressional Research Service or the Library of Congress, for which the author is a senior specialist working on nonproliferation matters and energy.

involvement in shaping nonproliferation policies has been characterized by periods of intense interest and activity interspersed with longer periods of little visible activity. By legislation Congress established the agencies most directly concerned with nonproliferation, notably the former Atomic Energy Commission (AEC) and its successors, the Energy Research and Development Administration (ERDA), the Department of Energy (DOE), and the Nuclear Regulatory Commission (NRC), and also the Arms Control and Disarmament Agency (ACDA). Congress mandated the nonproliferation policies in the Atomic Energy Act of 1946, and those that now appear in the Atomic Energy Act of 1954 as subsequently amended. Congress also has carved out for itself opportunities to participate, if it chooses, in certain decisions of the president and federal agencies relating to proliferation, but to date has not used these opportunities to overturn decisions of the executive branch.

Congress sees proliferation as a great threat to national security and world peace. In Congress's view a nation that does not already possess nuclear weapons should not undertake to enrich plutonium or store spent fuel. Instead, these services should be provided by international or multinational organizations. Ideally, reprocessing of spent nuclear fuel, recycling of plutonium, and further development of plutonium breeders in nonnuclear states should be prevented. Nuclear states should not provide the exports or technical assistance that will enable nonnuclear states to acquire enrichment or reprocessing capabilities. All nations should put their nuclear fuel cycles under the safeguards of the International Atomic Energy Agency (IAEA) and adhere to the Non-Proliferation Treaty (NPT). International safeguards should be improved to assure timely detection of dangerous diversions of nuclear materials. Some members of Congress would have the president negotiate an international agreement with other nations to apply sanctions against any state that violates or abrogates safeguards or nonproliferation commitments.

In recent years Congress has become distrustful of the executive's commitment to nonproliferation. The feeble American response to India's test explosion in 1974, the failure to stop the sale of reprocessing plants and equipment to Pakistan by France and to Brazil by West Germany, and the failure of American efforts to persuade potentially dangerous nations to ratify the NPT, coupled until recently with a father-knows-best attitude, have generated a congressional desire to take the lead in formulating the United States' nonproliferation policy and ensuring that the executive branch takes effective action.

In the age of Arthur Schlesinger's "Imperial Presidency," it was often fashionable to cast Congress as a subordinate in such international affairs as arms control and nonproliferation. The presidency is seen by some to possess a tightly focused expert wisdom that can better anticipate and handle problems than the confederated organization of the legislative branch. Without debating the general truth of this proposition, I would point out that sometimes Congress can run ahead of the executive in both anticipation and action.

The Era of Secrecy: 1946-1954

The nuclear era opened with radical American proposals for international control of atomic energy that went far beyond anything since adopted. As Soviet opposition stymied the proposals for international control of atomic energy made by U.S. Ambassador Bernard Baruch to the United Nations Atomic Energy Commission, Congress worked on the Atomic Energy Act of 1946, intended to preserve the secret of the atom bomb. As the United States demobilized after World War II, it stepped up development and production of nuclear weapons. Concern about proliferation was expressed by some, but was seen as academic. The public was delighted that nuclear weapons had rendered a bloody assault on Japan unnecessary. Nuclear scientists were lionized by society and listened to respectfully by high officials and legislators. By the late 1940s it was evident that secrecy had not prevented the Soviet Union from acquiring nuclear weapons. So in the early 1950s secrecy and noncooperation were relaxed by legislation.

The Atomic Energy Act of 1946 forged American nonproliferation policy for a decade. Much of the act was intended to prevent the spread of nuclear weapons by imposing secrecy, cutting off international cooperation, and subjecting possible private use of atomic energy to extraordinary controls. Since the Atomic Energy Act of 1946 was far more a creation of Congress than of the Truman administration, it is pertinent to identify those provisions intended to prevent proliferation.

The act made it national policy to control the dissemination of restricted data so as to assure the common defense and security.[1] It laid down two guiding principles, one virtually precluding any exchange of information on industrial uses of nuclear energy, the other holding open the exchange of scientific and technical information. The two principles were spelled out as follows:

1. That until Congress declares by joint resolution that effective and enforceable international safeguards against the use of atomic energy for destructive purposes have been established, there shall be no exchange of information with other nations with respect to the use of atomic energy for industrial purposes; and

2. That the dissemination of scientific and technical information relating to atomic energy should be permitted and encouraged so as to provide that free interchange of ideas and criticisms which is essential to scientific progress.

Note the absolute control retained by Congress over exchange of atomic information for industrial purposes on the one hand, and unfettered freedom for exchange of scientific and technical information on the other.

The act established extraordinary control over nuclear materials, primarily because of concern about proliferation, internal as well as foreign. It was unlawful for any person to own fissionable materials,[2] or to possess, use, or transfer them, except as licensed by the AEC. Against the possibility that individuals or organizations might help foreign organizations with nuclear energy, the act forbade any person or organization to engage directly or indirectly in the production of any fissionable material outside the United States. No person could own, transfer, deliver, or export uranium or other source materials unless licensed by the AEC. Congress also prohibited the manufacture, production, or export of any equipment or device utilizing fissionable material except by an AEC license. Here an unusual opportunity for congressional participation was built into the legislation. The act required that whenever the AEC believed any industrial, commercial, or other nonmilitary use of atomic energy was sufficiently developed to be of practical value, it was to report this to the president, who in turn was to report to Congress. The AEC had to provide an estimate of the social, economic, and international effects of such use, together with recommedations for legislation. No commercial license for any manufacture, production, export, or use could be issued by the AEC until a report had been filed and ninety days had elapsed while Congress was in session.

By 1951 foreign pressures caused some loosening of the secrecy and cutoff of international cooperation imposed by the 1946 act. The United States needed uranium from Canada and the Belgian Congo, while these countries, in turn, wanted access to some of the AEC's work in nuclear power. So Congress amended the 1946 act to allow ways of furnishing information to other countries. It authorized the AEC to enter into specific arrangements involving the communication of restricted data on refining, purification, and subsequent treatment of source materials; reactor development; production of fissionable materials; and related research and development. The five members of the AEC had to find unanimously that national security would be substantially promoted, not endangered, and that the arrangement met five additional statutory conditions.[3] At the time, virtually all information about commercial use of nuclear power had been classified as restricted data. The amendment also moderated the ban on direct or indirect assistance by Americans in foreign production of nuclear materials; the AEC was permitted to authorize such activities upon a determination by the president that national security would not be adversely affected.

The Era of Cooperation: 1954-1968

The era of nuclear secrecy and noncooperation ended suddenly, even as the Cold War was growing more chill and the Soviet Union assailed the United States for preoccupation with nuclear weapons. The end was signalled by President Eisenhower's Atoms for Peace proposal to the United Nations in December 1953, and was completed when Congress rewrote national nuclear policy in the Atomic Energy Act of 1954. Now, in a marked shift, U.S. policy combined promotion of nuclear power at home with cooperation abroad. The following decade saw the executive branch establish the network of bilateral agreements for nuclear cooperation that sustains our commercial nuclear relations today, as well as congressional authorization for U.S. participation in the IAEA and joint research and development with Euratom. This was an era of optimism about the future of nuclear power and friendly international cooperation. Congress continued some restrictions and reserved for itself continued opportunity to take part in certain key decisions.

In 1954 Congress, primarily at its own initiative, rewrote the nation's atomic energy legislation. The Atomic Energy Act of 1954 opened the way for domestic development of nuclear energy and greater international cooperation. The Eisenhower administration did not propose legislation to implement its Atoms for Peace proposal. It was congressional enthusiasm for international cooperation, under specified conditions, that led to provisions favoring international nuclear trade and cooperation. The following provisions of the 1954 act are especially pertinent to nuclear proliferation.

Criteria for declassification of restricted data were loosened by changing the required determination in the 1946 act that publication would not *adversely affect* the common defense and security to a determination that publication would not *cause undue risk* to the common defense and security. While seemingly a minor change, it led to a great surge of declassification. Tight control on the exchange of restricted data was retained. Until effective and enforceable international safeguards against destructive uses of atomic energy are established, there could be no unrestricted exchange of restricted data except as authorized by the president.[4] Any communication had to be under a cooperative agreement. Communication of restricted data relating to the design or fabrication of atomic weapons remained prohibited. The AEC remained the sole owner of fissionable materials until 1964 when a law was passed permitting private ownership. Widening the trail for international cooperation opened in 1951, Congress authorized agreements for cooperation with other nations or regional defense organizations under specific conditions and mandatory provisions.[5] Initially agreements for cooperation had to lie before a congressional committee for a specified time. Later, as the purpose of agreements changed from nuclear research to nuclear power, Congress required that agreements involving reactors above a certain size (five megawatts thermal energy) lie before Congress for a longer period and that a resolution be passed endorsing or opposing the agreement. This power tool has lain idle; no such agreements have been rejected by Congress.

As for cooperation with international organizations, the act authorized the president to enter into arrangements with a group of nations (e. g., Euratom) providing for international cooperation in nonmilitary applications of atomic energy, but only under an agreement for cooperation.

The AEC was given general authorization to distribute fissionable materials to nations or groups of nations. No limit was set for distribution to individual nations, but distribution to the IAEA or to other groups of nations could only be in such amounts and for such times as Congress authorized.

The new emphasis upon cooperation contemplated expanding nuclear exports, with conditions attached. In the 1954 act, Congress authorized the AEC to license export of nuclear materials and equipment to countries with which we had an agreement for cooperation, subject to an AEC determination that a proposed export of nuclear materials was not inimical to national security, or a proposed export of nuclear equipment would not constitute an unreasonable risk to national security. As for the control of technical assistance by persons or organizations, the authority to approve such cooperation was shifted from the president to the AEC, and made conditional upon a finding that the assistance would not entail undue risk to security.

In 1957 Congress authorized U.S. participation in the IAEA, with some restrictions. The AEC could distribute to the agency or to any group of nations only such amounts of fissionable materials and for such periods of time as were authorized by Congress. In reporting the legislation, the Joint Committee on Atomic Energy said of this restriction that congressional authorization was desirable since these materials "will form the life blood of our country in the future for both defense and peacetime purposes." The joint committee said it did not wish to place unnecessary obstacles in the agency's path, but it believed Congress should examine future transfers to make certain that material was not distributed in such amounts as to deprive the United States of an element vital to its needs. While the House dropped this restriction, it was reinstated in the Senate. Senator John W. Bricker led the drive for this congressional control, arguing that it would not be a blow to Atoms for Peace, that the IAEA's safeguards were inadequate; and that after the agency had some operating experience, Congress could pass a general authorization. The Bricker Amendment was retained, with modifications extending its application to transfers to other international agencies.

The Era of the NPT: 1968-1977

The euphoria of international nuclear cooperation was not to last. By the mid 1960s, the United Kingdom and France had tested nuclear weapons, and the Soviet Union was in a nuclear weapons race with the United States. Widespread commercial use of nuclear energy implied spreading the industrial base needed to produce potentially dangerous nuclear materials. So the specter of proliferation thus reappeared. In response, the United States initiated the diplomatic drive that culminated in the Non-Proliferation Treaty (NPT), which the Senate approved in 1968. The treaty itself took effect in 1970. During the late 1960s and well into the 1970s, the American nuclear industry dominated the world nuclear market, and the U.S. government continued to be the primary supplier of uranium-enrichment services for non-Communist countries, maintaining this monopoly by underselling potential competitors. With faith in the NPT, Congress relaxed its concern over proliferation. This was the era of the Strategic Arms Limitation Talks with the Soviet Union, which culminated in the SALT I Treaty signed and ratified in 1972; the treaty limiting underground nuclear weapons tests, signed during the 1974 summit meeting in Moscow; and the treaty on peaceful underground nuclear explosions, signed in 1976.

Congressional concern over proliferation revived in 1974, and Congress soon ran ahead of the executive branch in seeking ways to prevent international trade in nuclear plants and fuel from increasing the risks of proliferation. Senator Abraham Ribicoff's publication in April 1974 of the Rosenbaum report on the risks of theft of nuclear materials by violent organizations, the publication of the Willrich-Taylor study on risks of nuclear theft, the Indian government's test of a so-called peaceful nuclear explosive in May 1974—all contributed to revived concern.[6] The feeble response of the United States to the Indian test as well as the announcements that France had contracted to sell fuel-reprocessing equipment to South Korea and Pakistan, and West Germany to sell enrichment and reprocessing equipment to Brazil, fanned this concern.

Some legislation with nonproliferation provisions had been enacted, and work on comprehensive nonproliferation legislation was almost completed in the Senate when Congress adjourned for the election campaign of 1976.

The 94th Congress (1975-76) ran ahead of the Ford administration in raising the alarm about disturbing evidence of proliferation and in considering ways of using enrichment services as leverage to obtain foreign commitments to stronger nonproliferation measures. Detailed, specific criteria for licensing of nuclear exports, diplomatic initiatives to secure new controls over international nuclear trade and assistance, sanctions for violators of nonproliferation commitments, and assurances of a reliable supply of nuclear goods and services by the United States were all advanced against a seemingly passive executive branch. In addition to starting work on comprehensive nonproliferation legislation, Congress completed legislation containing bits and pieces of nonproliferation policy. One act advised the president on nonproliferation. Another imposed economic sanctions against countries that supplied or received the means of enrichment or fuel reprocessing unless certain conditions were met. Still another increased funding for support of safeguards under the IAEA. None were vetoed by the president. Each was a distinct addition to the mosaic of laws, regulations, and actions that, taken together, constitute the nonproliferation policy of the United States.

On December 12, 1975, the Senate passed a resolution urging the president to take the lead in seeking stronger, more comprehensive international safeguards to assure a substantial, immediate reduction in the risk of diversion or theft of fissionable materials. The resolution also requested the president to seek restraint by nuclear supplier nations (then meeting in London) in the transfer of nuclear technology, and their cooperation in assuring that nuclear equipment and technology were transferred only under the most rigorous safeguards.

Much of the nonproliferation debate in Congress focused on using leverage to dissuade other nations from actions that might increase proliferation. Senator Stuart Symington added sanctions to the Foreign Assistance Act of 1961 by an amendment to the International Security and Arms Export Control Act of 1976. The Symington Amendment prohibited funding of certain kinds of assistance to nations that delivered or received any equipment, materials, or technology for enriching uranium or reprocessing nuclear fuel unless two conditions were met. First, the countries involved had to place all such items upon delivery under multilateral auspices and management when available, and second, the recipients had to enter agreements to place all such items and all other nuclear fuel and facilities under IAEA safeguards. The assistance to be cut off if these conditions were violated included economic and military assistance under the Foreign Assistance Act and the Arms Export Control Act. The Symington Amendment left the president some discretion, authorizing him to continue the prohibited assistance if he certified in writing to Congress that terminating it would have a serious adverse affect on vital U.S. interests, and that he had received reliable assurances that the country would not acquire or develop nuclear weapons or assist other nations to do so. The president's discretion, however, was not unfettered. The amendment further provided that Congress by joint resolution of both houses might terminate or restrict the assistance for a country to which the prohibition applied, or take any other action it deemed appropriate.[7]

During 1976 Senator John Glenn successfully amended the Foreign Assistance and Related Programs Appropriations of 1976 to earmark $1 million for the IAEA to use in strengthening its safeguards and inspections. This was in addition to the additional $1 million a year for five years already promised by President Ford for this purpose.

Congressional interest in nonproliferation was sustained by the interjection of this issue in the presidential campaign. On May 13, 1976, Jimmy Carter, in a nuclear policy address at the United Nations, warned of proliferation and of the limitations of IAEA safeguards. Nuclear energy, he said, headed the list of global challenges that call for new forms of international action. He suggested action be considered to meet the energy needs of all countries while limiting reliance on nuclear energy, to limit the spread of nuclear weapons, and to make the spread of peaceful nuclear power less dangerous. On September 25, 1976, at San Diego, he elaborated further, saying that as president he would take eleven steps to control proliferation, including a ban on domestic reprocessing and an end to foreign sales of enrichment or reprocessing equipment, along with diplomatic initiatives to create multinational enrichment and spent-fuel storage facilities and conversion of the American breeder project into a long-term, possibly multinational effort.[8]

In the closing days of the campaign, on October 28, President Ford issued a statement on nuclear policy and nonproliferation that announced decisions to accelerate diplomatic initiatives, in conjunction with nuclear supplier and customer nations, to control the spread of plutonium and the technologies for separating plutonium from nuclear fuel; and to change reprocessing policy so that the United States would not reprocess and recycle plutonium unless there was sound evidence that the world community could effectively overcome the associated risks of proliferation. Ford said that the United States and other nations could and should increase their use of nuclear power for peaceful purposes even if reprocessing and recycling of plutonium proved unacceptable.

The Era of Doubt and Change: 1977–

By the close of the 94th Congress in 1976, a spirit of doubt and distrust about proliferation clearly was abroad. Whereas in the early days of the NPT the presumption was that the treaty and international safeguards could give enough assurance for the United States to be relaxed about nuclear exports and technical assistance, this presumption now was challenged. Nuclear export licenses were held up and the Nuclear Regulatory Commission undertook a massive reexamination of proliferation implications of plutonium recycling. The main perceived risk of proliferation changed. Whereas the IAEA and the NPT were intended to deter governments from acquiring nuclear weapons, now the threat seemed to be the malevolent use of nuclear materials by violent groups. Critics of the NPT pointed to the fundamental flaws of easy withdrawal from its commitments and the absence of strong, automatic sanctions. Nonetheless, while many questioned the commitment of some nations to the NPT, it was presumed that other nations would apply the agreed-upon economic sanctions and that no country would risk them by breaking nonproliferation commitments. Despite faltering faith in treaties, the United States and other nuclear supplier nations turned to informal, unpublished agreements secretly arrived at to impose new conditions on nuclear trade. We have entered an era when Congress is inclined to ask whether states not having nuclear weapons might not legitimately acquire nuclear materials and facilities under IAEA safeguards and then be able to divert them to weapons, ignoring the NPT and attendant agreements.

The first six months of the 95th Congress in 1977 was a tumultuous time for nonproliferation policies. The Nuclear Energy Policy Study Group, funded by the Ford Foundation, issued a report in March that called for strong new nonproliferation measures. The Carter administration took initial steps toward that end, and Congress continued work on comprehensive nonproliferation legislation. At this writing it seems likely that Congress will pass a comprehensive nonproliferation bill that will be a three-way compromise between House, Senate, and the administration.

Because of their potential impact on control of proliferation, it is worthwhile to examine President Carter's initiatives in detail. In a major shift in nuclear policy, on April 7, 1977, Carter ended government support for the production of plutonium and called on other nations to join the United States in halting the use of plutonium for nuclear fuel.[9] On April 27 he announced additional nonproliferation policies and conditions and sent to Congress his proposed Nuclear Non-Proliferation Policy Act. The additional policy decisions included new conditions for nuclear export licenses and for newly negotiated agreements for cooperation; policies for the excutive branch to follow in making recommendations to the Nuclear Regulatory Commission on the export of sensitive items such as plutonium and highly enriched uranium, and in deciding whether to approve a request by another nation to retransfer fuel supplied by the United States to a third nation for reprocessing; and policies to improve U.S. reliability as a nuclear fuel supplier. Taken together, these measures would place the United States in a leadership position among nuclear suppliers and establish a strong nonproliferation policy. They represent a delicately balanced blend of *denials* for those items such as reprocessing plants which create so large a risk that their export should be avoided altogether; *controls* over those items and technologies required by ongoing nuclear power programs, where improved safeguards and conditions for physical security will substantially reduce their dangers; and *incentives* to gain the support of other nations, notably uranium resource assessment and guaranteed access to nonsensitive low-enriched uranium and spent fuel storage.[10] Subsequently, the administration expanded this statement as follows:

1. We will continue to embargo the export of enrichment and reprocessing plants from the United States;
2. We will avoid new commitments to export significant amounts of plutonium except for gram quantities for research and analytical use;

3. We will avoid new commitments to export significant quantities of highly enriched uranium except when the project is of exceptional merit and the use of low-enriched fuel or some other less weapons-usable material is clearly shown to be technically infeasible;

4. We will not approve any supply of highly enriched uranium greater than fifteen kilograms unless the President himself approved the export;

5. We will undertake efforts to identify projects and facilities which might be converted to low-enriched uranium from highly enriched uranium; and

6. We will take steps to minimize inventories of weapons-usable uranium abroad.[11]

Major nonproliferation policy bills were well along by the August 1977 recess. Of the three bills before Congress, one represented the views of the Carter administration, one those of the House Committee on International Relations, and one those of the two leading senators in nonproliferation legislation.[12] The bills showed a remarkable advance by the administration toward ideas that members of Congress began to formulate in 1974. Congress and the Carter administration were agreed that preventing further proliferation is a major problem for the United States, that stronger controls over international nuclear trade are necessary, that the present statutory criteria that guide the export licensing decisions of the Nuclear Regulatory Commission should be reworked and made more specific, and that the United States should act to strengthen the IAEA and its safeguards.

The bills all contemplated diplomatic initiatives to win the agreement of other countries to stronger export controls on nuclear trade, particularly for the sensitive technologies of reprocessing and enrichment. All the bills would try to prevent or control reprocessing of nuclear fuels exported from the United States. All sought to make the United States a more reliable trading partner for those nations that agree to our nonproliferation commitments. The congressional and administration bills parted company on implementation. The congressional approach was to apply pressure by stipulating that after a specific period, probably eighteen months, a new set of export criteria would come into force; these would in effect unilaterally halt many U.S. nuclear exports to countries dragging their feet on nonproliferation negotiations. The administration preferred to negotiate without the threat of mandatory export stoppages. As of the fall of 1977, informal negotiations between Congress and the administration were inconclusive. Congress seemed little inclined simply to enunciate nonproliferation goals and then depend wholly on the executive branch to find ways of implementing them. Rather, members of Congress wanted to have a role in implementing the new policies, even to the extent of a congressional veto over some decisions (which would be subject, in turn, to a presidential override). Whatever the outcome of these negotiations, the result will be a marked change from the nonproliferation policies of the amended Atomic Energy Act of 1954.

On February 24, 1977, Senator Frank Church and several colleagues introduced a resolution commending the president's intention to give diplomatic priority to pursuit of nonproliferation measures. As amended and passed on April 28, the resolution endorsed negotiations with world leaders to: (1) curb the spread of nuclear enrichment and reprocessing facilities; (2) achieve acceptance of nuclear safeguards; (3) explore international provision of nuclear fuel services; (4) agree on sanctions against nations seeking to acquire nuclear explosives; (5) strengthen the IAEA; and (6) act promptly on legislation setting forth U.S. nonproliferation policy.

A few days later, on May 3, the House passed an amended version of the Export-Import Bank Act, which contains two nonproliferation provisions. One requires that the Bank bring any nuclear-related loans to Congress for a twenty-five day consideration period and that a detailed nuclear proliferation statement be provided by ACDA and the secretary of state. The other requires the secretary of state to report to Congress and the Bank if he determines that any country has violated or abrogated an agreement for cooperation with the IAEA or with the United States, or that a country has detonated a nuclear explosive. The secretary is to name the offending country and the Bank is not to approve financial assistance for nuclear exports to that country unless the president finds it in the national interest for the Bank to do so and his finding has lain before Congress for twenty-five days.

For its part the Senate passed a simple three-month extension of the present Bank Act to allow time for hearings. So the outcome of the House nonproliferation conditions is not yet known. In a related measure the Senate on August 5 agreed to a nonproliferation amendment to the foreign assistance appropriations bill for 1978. The amendment provides that Export-Import Bank financing for nuclear exports would be denied any nonnuclear state that detonated a nuclear device after the new Bank Act takes effect. What will happen to these attempts to make nonproliferation a consideration in Export-Import Bank financing remains to be seen. The important point is they illustrate the variety of congressional initiatives in nonproliferation.

By the end of July Congress had completed revision of the economic sanctions it had imposed the year before in amending the Foreign Assistance Act. The new version requires economic sanctions to be imposed on countries that export or import the means for enrichment or reprocessing unless certain conditions are met, with the conditions slightly different according to whether enrichment or reprocessing is involved.[13] The new legislation also contains a one-year ban on use of any funds under the Foreign Assistance Act to finance the construction, operation, or maintenance of any nuclear power plant under an agreement for cooperation.

On July 12 the Senate passed the Energy Research and Development Administration authorization for Fiscal Year 1978 with several nonproliferation amendments. An amendment by Senator Glenn provided that no nuclear fuel may be exported directly or indirectly to supply a nuclear power reactor to a nonnuclear-weapons state that has not ratified the NPT and whose agreement for cooperation with the United States was submitted to Congress before October 1974, unless the first proposed export (after enactment of this bill) was first submitted to Congress under the amended Atomic Energy Act of 1954. Another amendment, by Senator James McClure, prohibited use of federal funds to repurchase, transport, or store any foreign spent nuclear fuel, directly or indirectly, unless expressly authorized by the annual authorizations bill for the Energy Research and Development Administration or Department of Energy, except for fuel sent to India under an export license already approved in June 1977.

Conclusion

Since the beginning of the nuclear era, Congress has at times seized the initiative and exerted notable influence on the shaping of nonproliferation policy. It has established goals, criteria, and procedures for nuclear cooperation with other countries, and has supported international treaty commitments and organization to reduce the risk of proliferation. It has given itself the opportunity to participate in certain decisions affecting nuclear cooperation with other countries, but has so far not overturned any arrangements concluded by the executive. The congressional nonproliferation initiatives appear linked with the drive of Congress to reassert itself vis-à-vis the president, and seem likely to continue despite the common political affiliation of the new president and the majority of Congress. The Carter administration therefore cannot expect its ideas on nonproliferation to be adopted quickly and without change. It can expect Congress to press for its own goals, policies, and measures to deal with proliferation. How great the resultant tensions between Congress and the executive will be remains to be seen. What can be said now is that without the interest of Congress and the pressures it has generated, it is unlikely that U.S. nonproliferation policies would be moving forward as they are today.

In the context of Congress and arms control, the case of nonproliferation provides a good example of the potential impact of congressional initiatives and influence. It also suggests the uncertainties caused by the variability of congressional attentiveness and the need for some way to sustain an effective working interest between peaks of congressional activity. Since the drive for nonproliferation legislation has come from members not usually associated with arms control legislation, analyzing their thinking about nonproliferation may suggest ways to enlist their support for other arms control measures, as well as gain the support of the arms control community for nonproliferation initiatives.

Notes

1. Restricted data were defined as all data concerning the manufacture or utilization of atomic weapons, the production of fissionable materials, or the use of fissionable material in the production of power; it did not include data that the AEC from time to time determined might be published without adversely affecting security.

2. Fissionable materials were defined as uranium enriched in the U-235 isotope, uranium-233, and plutonium.

3. No such arrangement could (a) involve the communication of restricted data on design and fabrication of atomic weapons; or (b) be entered into with any nation threatening the security of the United States; (c) the restricted data involved should be limited and circumscribed to the maximum degree consistent with the common defense and security objective in view, and the AEC had to determine that the recipient nation's security standards for such data were adequate; (d) the president, after securing the written recommendations of the National Security Council and incorporating them in his report, had to state in writing that the arrangement would substantially promote, not endanger, the security of the United States; and (e) before the arrangement was consummated, the Joint Committee on Atomic Energy was to be fully informed for a period of 30 days while Congress was in session.

4. The act limited such exchange to restricted data on: (a) refining, purification, and subsequent treatment of source material; (b) civilian reactor development; (c) production of special nuclear material; (d) health and safety; (e) industrial and other peaceful applications of atomic energy; and (f) related research and development.

5. The conditions were: (a) the AEC has to submit the proposed agreement to the president with its recommendations; (b) the president has to approve and authorize execution of the proposed agreement and make a written determination that "the performance of the proposed agreement . . . will not constitute an unreasonable risk to the common defense and security"; (c) the proposed agreement, together with the president's approval and determina-

tion, has to be submitted to the Joint Committee on Atomic Energy for 30 days before it takes effect.

In addition, Congress specified that each agreement must include: (a) the terms, conditions, duration, nature, and scope of the cooperation; (b) a guarantee by the cooperating party that security safeguards and standards agreed upon will be maintained; and (c) a guarantee by the cooperating party that no material or restricted data will be transferred to unauthorized persons or beyond the jurisdiction of the cooperating party except as specified in the agreement.

Congress later tightened its control over such agreements for cooperation by requiring them to lie before the Joint Committee for 60 days and providing that any such agreement would not take effect if, during this time, Congress passes a concurrent resolution opposing the proposed agreement.

6. For Rosenbaum report, *Congressional Record,* April 30, 1974, S-6630 (daily ed.). See also Mason Willrich and Theodore B. Taylor, *Nuclear Theft: Risks and Safeguards* (Cambridge, Mass., 1974).

7. A joint resolution requires no action by the president, so it is a veto-proof legislative act.

8. Carter's proposed steps were to: (a) call upon all nations to adopt a voluntary moratorium on the sale or purchase of enrichment or reprocessing plants, to apply retroactively to such agreements as those between Germany and Brazil, and France and Pakistan; (b) make no new commitments of nuclear technology or fuel to countries that refuse to forego nuclear explosives, refrain from national nuclear reprocessing, and place their nuclear facilities under IAEA safeguards; (c) seek to withhold authority for domestic commercial reprocessing until the necessity, economy, and safety of this technology are proved; any commercial reprocessing undertaken should be on a multinational basis; (d) call for an international conference on energy; (e) seek to renegotiate existing agreements for cooperation; (f) support a strengthening of the safeguards and inspection authority of the IAEA and place all U.S. nonmilitary nuclear facilities under those safeguards; (g) explore international initiatives such as multinational enrichment plants and multinational spent-fuel storage as alternatives to the establishment of enrichment or reprocessing plants on a national basis; (h) ensure that the U.S. is again a reliable supplier of enriched uranium by supporting enlargement of government-owned facilities; (i) redirect U.S. energy research and development to correct the disproportionate emphasis on nuclear power at the expense of renewable energy technologies; convert the breeder reactor project into a long-term,

possibly multinational effort; (j) negotiate a comprehensive test ban treaty with the Soviet Union and reduce, through SALT, strategic nuclear forces and technology; (k) encourage the Soviet Union to join the U.S. in a total ban of all nuclear explosives for at least five years, including so-called peaceful nuclear devices.

9. The president said the U.S. will: (a) defer indefinitely the commercial reprocessing and recycling of plutonium produced in U.S. nuclear power programs; (b) give greater priority to alternative designs for breeders using materials other than plutonium and defer the date when breeder reactors are put into commercial use; (c) direct funding of U.S. nuclear research and development programs to accelerate research into alternative nuclear fuel cycles that do not involve direct access to materials usable in nuclear weapons; (d) increase U.S. capacity to produce nuclear fuels—enriched uranium in particular—to provide adequate, timely supplies of nuclear fuels to other countries so they will not be required or encouraged to reprocess their own materials; (e) propose legislation to permit the U.S. to sign supply contracts and thus remove the pressure for the reprocessing of nuclear fuels by other countries; (f) continue to embargo the export of either equipment or technology that could permit uranium enrichment and chemical reprocessing; and (g) continue discussions with supplier and recipient countries of a wide range of international approaches and frameworks that will permit all countries to meet their energy needs while at the same time reducing the spread of nuclear explosive capability. *Presidential Documents* 13 (April 11, 1977): 503-4.

10. Ibid. (May 2, 1977): 611-13.

11. Statement of Joseph S. Nye, Jr., Department of State, before the Senate Committee on Foreign Relations, June 29, 1977.

12. The bills referred to include the Antiproliferation Act of 1977 as reported by the House Committee on International Relations, H.R. 8638; the Nuclear Non-Proliferation Act of 1977, as agreed to by Senators Charles Percy and John Glenn, S. 897; and the administration's Nuclear Non-Proliferation Policy Act, S. 1432 and H.R. 6910.

13. The International Security Assistance Act of 1977, as sent to the president on July 22, amended the Foreign Assistance Act of 1961. It adds a section to cut off funds under the International Security Assistance Act or the Arms Export Control Act of any country that delivers nuclear enrichment equipment, materials, or technology to any other country, or that receives such equipment, materials,

or technology from any other country, unless two conditions are met before delivery. First, the supplying and receiving countries must have agreed to place all such items upon delivery under multilateral auspices and management when available; second, the recipient country must have agreed with the IAEA to place all such items and also all nuclear fuel and facilities in the country under IAEA safeguards. The president may continue to furnish prohibited assistance if he certified in writing to Congress that the termination would have a serious adverse effect on vital U.S. interests, and that he has received reliable assurances that the country in question will not acquire or develop nuclear weapons or assist other nations in doing so. The bill also specifies procedures for Senate action on any joint resolution to terminate or restrict such assistance.

As for reprocessing, the bill adds a new section that also provides for the cutoff of funds specified above to any country that delivers nuclear reprocessing equipment, materials, or technology to any other country or receives such equipment, materials, or technology from any other country (except for the transfer of reprocessing technology associated with the investigation, under international evaluation programs in which the United States participates, of technologies that are alternatives to pure plutonium reprocessing), or is not a nuclear-weapons state under the NPT and detonates a nuclear explosive. The president may continue to furnish such assistance if he certifies in writing to Congress that the termination of such assistance would be seriously prejudicial to the common achievement of U.S. nonproliferation objectives or would otherwise jeopardize national security. The bill also specifies procedures for Senate action on any joint resolution to terminate or restrict the assistance.

8
Secrecy in Arms Control Negotiations

Lawrence D. Weiler

In recent years much of the important negotiation on arms control has taken place in an environment of excessive secrecy. The most critical negotiations, the Strategic Arms Limitation Talks (SALT), have been conducted with policy debates and decision making confined within a small segment of the executive branch.

Under President Carter, who advocated as a candidate and advocates as president a more open government, there has been a change from past practice, which excluded much of Congress and the public from effective knowledge of the SALT negotiations. Indeed, Mr. Carter is criticized in some quarters for having been "too open" in his first SALT effort. Encouraging as the initial moves toward openness of the new administration may be, however, there will be strong pressures both inside and outside of the government to revert to the closed pattern of the recent past.

It is the argument of this essay that we cannot afford a return to the secrecy-shrouded process of arms control negotiation

At the time this paper was written, the author was adjunct professor of political science at Stanford University. The editors express their appreciation to the Stanley Foundation for permission to draw upon the author's Stanley Foundation Occasional Paper no. 12, *The Arms Race, Secret Negotiations, and the Congress,* as the basis for this chapter.

that evolved in recent years. The ills of past practice resided in particular in the cloak of secrecy woven over public policy *during negotiations,* for that is when the real options develop, the crucial decisions are made, and the future course of events is largely determined. While Secretary of State Henry Kissinger followed a different course in practice, verbally he maintained that the executive and Congress had the joint responsibility to define the contours of a new world. He argued that our foreign policy cannot be effective if it reflects only the sporadic, esoteric initiatives of a small group of specialists.

Nowhere is this more true than in efforts to control the arms race, with its direct implications for security, perhaps survival, détente, and resource allocation. Any meaningful national discussion of the broader issues of détente and strategic policy requires a radical reduction in the obsessive secrecy so characteristic of foreign policy conduct in recent years. Nicholas Katzenbach has cogently analyzed the necessity of openness and candor if foreign policies are to have broad public support, which is essential to their effectiveness and the compatibility of policymaking with our democratic principles.[1] Not only have Vietnam, Watergate, and other recent national traumas taught us something about the consequences of secrecy and the corrosive effects of decision making within small, closed groups; the skepticism they have produced has made openness all the more indispensable if national politics of broad import are to have the necessary backing of a significant majority of our citizens. And without such backing, bold foreign policy initiatives may be precluded, and our government forced to seek accommodation within a narrow set of parameters. Hard decisions and real policy choices are seldom made at the initiation of negotiations.

Yet somehow it became accepted, particularly among the professionals—practitioners and writers alike—that arms control negotiations, and particularly SALT, constituted a special area that should be shielded from public view and real congressional scrutiny. A myth that is too widely and uncritically accepted is that of the overwhelming necessity of total secrecy in arms negotiations (the preferred euphemism is privacy). It is not argued here that privacy in negotiations is a superseded relic of the past. Formal and informal private explorations of possible compromises should, and of course will, continue to play an important role in arms control diplomacy. The exact optimum balance between privacy and openness in arms control efforts will not be easy to set. But a significant improvement over the conditions of the past can be made long before the ideal balance has been determined. In all of this the role of Congress is central, for Congress is the principal agent through which more openness and greater public participation can be brought about.

Examining the patterns of the past and their consequences may be helpful in determining our future course. From 1969 to 1976 the secrecy of the SALT negotiations became equated by most skeptics and arms controllers alike with the talks' "seriousness." Similar thinking persists today in some quarters. One effect of this has been to corrupt the language of public discourse. In a call for demystification of American foreign policy, Norman Cousins pointed to officials' "fascination with obscurantism and abstractions," and argued that "the public discussion by officials of foreign policy is so full of murky language and gobbledygook that it is losing all connection with the American people."[2] Arms control is perhaps the leading victim of official obscurantism.

With a few exceptions secrecy and the exclusion of all but a select few from policy input was the rule. (The ABM issue in the SALT I negotiations is a possible exception, a matter I discuss later for the lessons it may teach.) The occasional leaks that appeared in the press during negotiations, some accurate, some not, and most dealing with but fragments of the total picture, did not alter the basic situation.[3] It is instructive to reflect on some facts concerning the period before 1977. The *texts* of the various proposals submitted to the Soviet Union by the United States during SALT I and II were not shown to the Congress, even in executive session, let alone made available for public comment. U.S. proposals, even in nontextual form, were not available for scrutiny by Congress as a whole or by the public. Specific counterproposals submitted by the Soviets were never made available for public assessment.

The degree of secrecy surrounding strategic arms control

efforts until 1977 had several adverse effects. The professional community's contribution to public and congressional discussion of means to halt the arms race was significantly lessened. The traditional role of the press in maintaining an informed and involved citizenry nearly ceased to exist. Congress could not perform its proper role in policy formulation and in ensuring executive accountability. Arms control efforts were hurt, not helped. And there was, in this area, a not inconsiderable abridgment of the democratic process.

One adverse consequence of excessive secrecy is that the attention of strategy and arms control analysts outside government has tended to move away from critical discussion of the specifics of ongoing arms control negotiations, and to focus instead on such matters as the general problem of deterrence, the pros and cons of particular weapons systems, strategic doctrine and weapons requirements, the causes of strategic arms competition, and the present and future status of the strategic balance between the United States and the Soviet Union. These are important subjects; they obviously have a significant bearing on arms control issues and on unilateral actions by the United States aimed at increasing strategic stability, maintaining a secure deterrent force, and avoiding wasteful expenditures. Yet if one compares the intellectual effort and detailed analyses the professional community has devoted to such subjects with the absence of specific analysis of strategic arms control options directly relevant to ongoing negotiations, the contrast is striking.

The general paucity of discussion about specific arms control solutions is true not only of the professional and academic community, but of the news media as well. In news stories and editorial comments on SALT during past negotiations, one could not fail to notice that, when the sentences began to approach the proposals or options at the heart of the negotiations, the words usually dissolved into meaningless generalities, generalities that precluded rational public discourse.

If public discourse tended to become sterile from lack of information, was the situation no better within Congress? The executive branch did, after all, brief the leadership and certain committees during the SALT negotiations. But while some members of Congress obviously had access to more information than the public, the situation there was, if anything, even more serious. Congress is the institution responsible for ensuring that, with the aid of the press, a broad public discussion of public issues brings into play the array of talent and wisdom outside the executive branch. At least so far as arms control and strategy were concerned, we seemed to have forgotten that this is one of the vitalizing features of representative government. Moreover, we delegate responsibility to members of Congress to appraise alternative courses of action and allocate public money on the assumption that they will be informed. Their being inadequately informed in the past during SALT negotiations meant they could not exercise their responsibilities in this area. In what other area of comparable import would we have tolerated a situation in which, if a constituent asked his congressman's opinion on the government's proposals, the people's elected representative was forced to reply, "I do not know what they are"?

Executive branch spokesmen operated under what were, in effect, White House instructions to avoid serious discussion of most of the issues under debate within the executive branch and not to volunteer details that would reveal the administration's real positions. Such congressional briefings as there were tended to be after-the-fact reporting and were usually structured at White House direction to conceal many of the critical issues under debate within the political-military bureaucracy that arises during a negotiation. The transcripts of these classified hearings, moreover, were available only to committee members and did not include texts of proposals. Under such conditions, there can be little real collaboration in developing national policies. Nor under such a system can there be an honest exchange between government and citizen.

There are some who would argue that much of the fault lay with Congress. Many of the oral briefings in executive sessions were in fact quite detailed, but many committee members showed little interest in pursuing points that would have uncovered "hookers" in the administration's position, or in pressing for discussion of alternative options (usually under debate within the executive branch at the time) that might have brought the Soviet Union and United States together. There is some validity in this description if not in the line of argument; how frequently in recent years did one hear those hoping an issue would receive ventilation outside the closed debate of the executive branch exclaim, "If only they would ask the right questions!" But this is a case where not only do two wrongs not make a right, but where the first wrong makes the second more likely.

No meaningful consultation with Congress can occur when specific proposals are not available, when such information as is provided is not accessible for study and reflection, when Congress is largely denied the right of staff access for analysis, and, most important, when such interchange between the two branches of government as does occur takes place only before negotiations when general opening positions are discussed, or in a subsequent review of results of a particular negotiating session produced by the key decisions made during the course of negotiations, or after a particular negotiating session has produced a publicizable result, a *fait accompli.* Kissinger's impressive abilities as a briefer, particularly at congressional leadership meetings at the White House, may have given a select few the sense of being informed; but neither his briefings nor those conducted before committees by lesser officials alter the fact that none of the requirements for real consultation were being met.

The argument for more openness in arms control negotiations is in a general sense an argument for a return to the situation more like that which existed before the 1969-76 period rather than a call for a radical departure from traditional practice. While efforts to keep Congress and the public at arm's length were not totally unknown before 1969, arms control negotiations have been conducted with the nation aware of the position of its government and even of specific texts of its proposals. The Nuclear Test Ban Treaty and the Non-Proliferation Treaty negotiations are two examples; they involved important and often contentious issues.

During both the test ban and nonproliferation negotiations, there were frequent consultations with Congress, and texts of key articles were often discussed with members of relevant committees before their submission to the Soviets. During both these negotiations, the Senate, in the 1963 Humphrey-Dodd Resolution on a limited test ban and the 1966 Pastore Resolution on nonproliferation, made a significant contribution to the success of these efforts; in part this resulted from the strong political support these resolutions gave officials in the executive branch who favored further sustained efforts when negotiations seemed at an impasse.

Some awareness of deficiencies in arrangements and procedures predated President Carter's efforts to alter his predecessors' practices. They were reflected in testimony before the Subcommittee on National Security Policy and Scientific Developments. Dean Rusk, for example, observed: "When we talk about limitation of arms, we are in a field which has a very specific and direct bearing upon the constitutional powers of the Congress to raise armies, provide for the national defense, maintain a Navy, and so forth, and I think that the limitation of arms field might be somewhat like the trade field, a field shared between the Senate and the House of Representatives, more than has been done in the past."[4] Fred Iklé maintained that the legislative branch must share with ACDA the task of being the "conscience" of U.S. policy on arms control and disarmament; one reason why this should be, he argued, was that "the key decisions and basic choices must be open to the American Public."[5] A more direct prescription for achieving this goal, however, is McGeorge Bundy's observation (made in the context of improving congressional consideration of the arms control impact of new weapons systems but equally applicable to arms control negotiations) that "the answer here lies in the provision of a sufficient base of information . . . to permit the Congress to formulate its own views and to take an adversary position with respect to the Executive branch."[6] In observing that it was possible to recall "painful experiences over the past ten years, at least [those in] which the Administration has thought of this kind of information in a proprietary way and in an instrumental way, to such a degree that the process of communication with the Congress on issues in which the Congress and the public had a right to information was severely constricted," Bundy pointed to what is probably an essential political requirement for change: "The kinds of access that we are speaking of here are not possible except in an atmosphere in which there is genuine acceptance of the proposition that except for the process of decision making itself, an Administration assumes a greater obligation of openness in sharing its information and explaining its decisions."[7]

Among those who perceive the need for greater openness, as the Carter administration begins to develop its own policies in this regard, there will be differing views regarding the nature and extent of change required. Some suggestions are offered here.

The basic proposals of the United States government should be available to Congress and to the public. The *texts* of such proposals should be available at least to the appropriate congressional committees and their staffs. The issues involved in policy alternatives and considerations bearing on them should be discussed with congressional committees and, to the extent mutually acceptable to those committees and the executive branch, be made part of the public record, "sanitized" if necessary to remove sensitive technical information regarding weapons or technical intelligence. Key issues, including Soviet counterproposals, that develop in the course of negotiations should be discussed with the appropriate congressional committees on a regular basis and, at a minimum, before executive branch decisions stemming from those issues and counterproposals are made. Major changes in American positions during negotiations should not remain the exclusive property of the executive long after they have been brought to the negotiating table. Without obviating the above considerations, the privacy of formal and informal exchanges between the two SALT delegations and higher-level officials should continue to be preserved.

Such changes may exceed or fall short of what is finally determined to be the right balance, and that balance may itself require time and experience to establish, and may also change over time. The first and most significant step, however, is a firm national decision that the earlier degree of secrecy surrounding the SALT process must be reduced. There is and will continue to be strong resistance to such change, as is reflected in the initial reactions to Mr. Carter's efforts to open up the process. This essay is intended as at least a partial brief for such efforts.

The first argument advanced for maintaining any arrangement is that is has worked effectively in achieving its stated purpose. This is not the sole standard of judgment, for questions of principle may by involved as in the present case. However, if we measure what has been achieved in SALT by this standard, we should assess not only the overall results but also how the positive and negative elements of those results relate to the practice of secrecy.

If we measure past SALT negotiations in terms of their effectiveness in controlling (1) strategic defensive arms and (2) strategic offensive arms, the readings are sharply divergent. In the case of defensive arms there was a major success. In the case of offensive arms there was a failure—a failure that cannot be explained merely by pointing to the greater complexities involved. The results of SALT negotiations conducted under great secrecy do not argue against change; they argue for it. This is true of both the major positive result and the major negative result.

The two major strategic weapons developments of the past decade that have been perceived as threatening strategic stability, that have been the principal catalysts of (or arguments used to support) the strategic arms competition and have been the central SALT issues, are the ABM (Antiballistic Missile) and MIRVs (Multiple Independently Targetable Reentry Vehicles). The former has for all practical purposes been effectively controlled through the ABM Treaty and its subsequent protocol. However, the failure in SALT I to ban MIRVs for offensive forces,[8] with the subsequent astronomically high MIRV levels permitted under the Vladivostok Accord, constitutes the great tragedy of SALT, with its full consequences for the taxpayer and for strategic stability yet to be reckoned. These two divergent results of SALT are directly related to the issue of secrecy.

In the case of the ABM, there was an extensive public and congressional debate before SALT opened, a debate that continued as SALT began and that produced a real if not specifically articulated political consensus outside the executive branch. While the Nixon administration "won" the great ABM debate in the Senate when Vice-President Spiro Agnew cast the tie-breaking vote for the Safeguard ABM program, it became increasingly clear that Safeguard was, in the words of one high official, "a busted flush." Public airing of the issues surrounding the Safeguard program produced enough opposition to deployment—on technical, strategic, and arms control grounds—that only the bargaining chip argument could keep the program alive. In a broad sense a major arms control issue had been decided in open discussion among a much wider group than the usual small circle of executive branch officials. The severe SALT limitations imposed on ABMs flowed directly from this open national discussion—as well, of course, as the Soviets' interest in such an outcome. When such an interest was indicated very early in SALT I, the limitation of ABMs in any agreement to such low levels as would render them ineffective in both fact and perception was close to inevitable.[9]

Thus the cloak of secrecy imposed on SALT had less effect on ABMs than it did on efforts to limit offensive arms. Without such secrecy, however, there would have been more likelihood of a total ABM ban, an option of interest to the Soviets during the later stages of SALT I.

The effort to control MIRVs was a different story. In this case the pressures for deployment had free rein within the protected, closed environment that secret negotiations afford. Congress had to some extent exhausted itself in the great ABM debate, and efforts to develop a comparable public debate on MIRVs before SALT I began never quite got off the ground. Some committee hearings were held,[10] and some congressmen discussed a moratorium on MIRV testing and deployment. But the general disposition was to let the negotiations begin without outside intervention, particularly after the administration let it be known that qualitative limitations, including controls on MIRVs, would be explored by the United States.

The nature of the administration's MIRV ban proposal, however, was never disclosed to the public or to most members of Congress, and those members who did receive oral briefings never fully understood the government's position. Letting it be known that a MIRV ban proposal had been advanced deflected opposition to MIRVs outside the executive branch. Yet the specifics of the proposal were such that rejection by the Soviets was inevitable. (Whether the proposal was constructed as it was to defer a decision on a MIRV ban or whether it represented a firm decision not to make a real effort to stop MIRVs remains a matter of conjecture.) In addition to calling for a MIRV test ban—which, though it would have precluded the Soviets from attaining a MIRV technology, was then regarded as the essential means of assuring that no MIRVs would be deployed—it called for on-site inspection of strategic missiles, and also on-site verification of any ABM limitation. Further, the proposal would have permitted the United States to continue producing and stockpiling MIRVs as long as they were not deployed.[11] Finally, the proposal was presented as an inseparable part of the United States's opening proposal on limiting offensive weapons, which included limitations not only on central strategic systems but also on Soviet Intermediate- and Medium-Range Ballistic Missiles.

The Soviet MIRV proposal included a production and deployment ban. It made no mention of a test ban, but throughout SALT I the Soviets conspicuously avoided official rejection of a test ban. This was a critical juncture in the effort to control strategic arms. Yet with secrecy concealing the issues and developments in the negotiations, knowledge of this crucial opportunity was confined within a closed group and allowed to lapse.

SALT I negotiations on specific proposals did not begin until mid April 1970. While unaware of the real nature of the administration's MIRV proposal, many members of the Senate, led by Senator Edward Brooke, were concerned that our ongoing MIRV program would foreclose any chance to stop this new system. Unable to consider the specifics of the MIRV negotiations, the Senate passed a resolution (211), calling generally for a quick, standstill freeze on further deployments by both sides of defensive and offensive strategic weapons. This occurred in May. In mid June a recess was called in the SALT negotiations to assess the results of the initial proposals and subsequent exchanges. The "forward-based systems" question raised early on by the Soviets was the offensive arms issue that received most attention. The critical issue within the administration, however, was how or even whether the MIRV negotiation would be pursued. In July the White House decided to advance a more limited proposal for offensive arms limitation, one that excluded limitations on MIRVs. Although administration spokesmen maintained in congressional briefings and in public comments that efforts to achieve limitations on MIRVs would continue, the July decision in fact meant that the effort to stop MIRVs had been abandoned, after just two months of actual negotiations!

While some individuals within the executive branch made periodic attempts to get a decision allowing serious negotiation on MIRVs to start, the secrecy of the negotiations meant that potential supporters outside the executive branch could not be effectively mobilized.[12] No new MIRV proposal was ever put to the Soviets, though throughout SALT I, behind the curtain of secrecy, the controversy continued over whether to make a real effort on MIRVs.

Perhaps Moscow would never have agreed to a MIRV test ban even if a revised MIRV proposal, separated from other elements of the comprehensive package, had been advanced, though some senior officials within the executive believed the odds sufficiently good to make the effort worthwhile. Even if Moscow had insisted on acquiring a MIRV technology, a serious negotiation might have disclosed that future Soviet MIRV plans involved not MIRVing existing missiles (which was the assumption in Washington and the basis for the U.S. proposal to ban further testing), but rather developing, new, larger missiles which would require verifiable silo modifications (and which now forms the basis for the counting rule for MIRV limitations in the SALT II accord). It is ironic, and perhaps instructive, that after Vladivostok, Secretary Kissinger said he wished the government had thought through the implications of a MIRVed world. In any event, the effort was not made; the Soviets, concluding that Washington had advanced its MIRV ban proposal merely to satisfy domestic opinion and faced with a proposal that involved no restrictions on any United States strategic program then planned, lost interest in early limitations on offensive arms almost immediately after the United States presented its revised proposal excluding MIRV limitations. A few weeks later the Soviets began to talk about focusing initially on ABMs, which became the formal Soviet position later in the year.

What can we conclude from this arms control failure? The country and the Congress were deceived about the *bona fides* of their government's efforts to halt MIRVs. When the White House decision of July was taken—a critical decision in efforts to control strategic arms—Congress and the public were precluded by the cloak of secrecy from any participation in that decision. Finally, the secrecy of the negotiations, which prevented the application of a wider spectrum of analysis and wisdom (as well as pressure), directly contributed to the major arms control failure of SALT. The abandonment of MIRV control efforts in SALT I was followed, in the still secrecy-shrouded negotiations that led to the Vladivostok Accord, by failure to seek what was still technically possible—either a phased program for a de-MIRVed world or a very low ceiling on MIRVed forces.

Yet, even though secrecy has been counterproductive for arms control efforts, those who feel more comfortable with secret negotiations will probably seize upon the initial difficulties of the Carter administration's new approach to argue for a return to a closed process. Let us look at the arguments for secret negotiations most likely to be put forward. I believe they lack either sufficient validity or sufficient weight to defeat the case for a more open process.

1. *The Soviets want secret negotiations and have complained about breaches of privacy in SALT.*

True. However, this point had more relevance at the very beginning of SALT, when the talks were exploratory discussions and when the Vietnam conflict left the Soviets highly sensitive about conducting bilateral talks with the United States and undecided about entering actual negotiations.

But SALT has long since become an established process. Soviet preferences, moreover, cannot be allowed, or used as an excuse, to alter the proper functioning of our system of government, which is precisely what happens when vital issues of public policy are secretly debated within a small circle throughout negotiations that will continue for years. That should be the controlling consideration on this point for the United States. We should also be aware that the Soviets' preference for secrecy may serve their interests, but not those of the United States. For example, the greater the degree of secrecy that surrounds SALT, the greater the psychological assist to the idea of condominium and the greater the consequent feeling of exclusion among our allies, an effect that can be offset only partially by periodic, restricted briefings. Moreover, a Soviet preference—and admittedly it is a strong one—is not the same as a Soviet condition, as the history of postwar arms negotiations demonstrates. Like other states, the USSR negotiates seriously when it is in its interest to do so. And the Soviets have not been hesitant to acknowledge that SALT, for a variety of reasons we can share, is in their interest.

2. *Secrecy is necessary because SALT involves, on both sides, very sensitive matters of strategic policy and strategic weapons.*

These words have an ominously impressive sound, but they lack real meaning. The strategic force structures and capabilities of the United States and the Soviet Union, as well as projections regarding future developments, are not secret.[13] The extensive public treatment of these matters in the annual Posture Statement of the secretary of defense is more detailed than the basic analysis of SALT proposals requires.[14] And the available public data are more detailed than those developed in the private exchanges between the two SALT delegations— though, as indicated earlier, I do not suggest that the privacy of such exchanges be ended.

Moreover, no third-party issues affecting critical arms limitations choices have arisen in SALT that are not a matter of public record. In any event, should the need for private talks on such matters arise in the future, present arrangements for the meetings between the two delegations and for high-level back channel exchanges should suffice.

3. *More public airing of issues arising in negotiations leads to more propaganda exchanges and precludes serious negotiation.*

This is a widely held view in the diplomatic community and one that observers have tended to accord more credence than it deserves, at least in the field of arms control. It is true that when plenary sessions of a negotiating forum are open, there is a somewhat greater tendency to play to the gallery and to indulge in polemics. The privacy of the SALT delegations' exchanges probably has contributed to the moderate tone which has characterized that forum, and this arrangement need not be modified. But the view that the almost total secrecy imposed on SALT was responsible for a unique seriousness and absence of polemics is in part false and in part overdrawn. This was largely due to two misconceptions.

The first concerns the supposed uniqueness of SALT with respect to serious, nonpolemical exchanges. Such exchanges in arms control negotiations preceded SALT and occurred in conditions of openness that were not greatly different from those advocated earlier in this article.[15] The tone of private exchanges during the negotiations on the Non-Proliferation Treaty, for example, and the "businesslike" conduct of those negotiations were not significantly different, yet in that case the areas of agreement and disagreement were more widely known, to Congress and to the public. There is no public evidence that the greater openness of the Carter administration has changed the nature of private discussions since Secretary of State Cyrus Vance's initial visit to Moscow.

The second misconception is that polemics and propaganda of a kind that interferes with negotiations are caused primarily by public exposure to the issues and the positions of the parties. There is little evidence in the postwar history of arms negotiations to support this view. What that history does indicate is that the level of polemics and propaganda is directly related to the general political climate, the expectation of serious negotiations, or both. When the political climate improves, public polemics decline, and even if some persist, they usually are not allowed to interfere with serious negotiations. While the point should not be pressed too far, it is nevertheless true that even when the political climate is conducive to polemics, if the desire for agreement *and* the expectation of a serious negotiation are present, verbal excesses are not allowed to interfere with serious negotiations.[16]

All this is not to say that when issues are in the public domain, the parties will not make their case, at times rather strongly; this uses up time. But, contrary to another of the myths that has grown up around SALT, that forum has not escaped the apparent need to engage in time-consuming debates "for the record" that contribute little to substantive negotiations. Such time-consuming debates of this nature are sometimes a nuisance, but they do not really interfere with serious negotiations, which in many cases proceed simultaneously.

4. Congressional and public knowledge of the United States proposal tends to freeze our positions, making more difficult the inevitable adjustments and compromises.

There may be an element of truth in this argument, but there is little evidence in the history of postwar arms negotiations to suggest that it has affected *important* modifications of position, except in a few cases where modification would have been in a direction opposed by a large segment of the Congress. Perhaps the most important such instance was the strong feeling in the Senate in 1963 that the United States should hold firm regarding on-site inspection for any comprehensive nuclear test ban. This case, however, illustrates an important point. The restraint on flexibility caused by strongly held congressional views stems primarily from the Constitutional requirement that two-thirds of the Senate must approve a treaty. This consideration applies whether the negotiations leading to a treaty are enclosed in secrecy or are more open.[17]

Any increased congressional restraint on flexibility under a more open process is likely to be offset by a reduction in such restraint within the executive branch, a reduction that will occur when arms control supporters outside the present system exercise some influence. And, in any event, a more direct and open dialogue between the two branches of government is likely to demonstrate that congressmen understand the need for give and take in achieving mutually acceptable solutions; it is when they are excluded from the action that they are most likely to react with seemingly inflexible stances.

Greater flexibility, moreover, is not always a virtue, from the standpoint either of United States interests or of effective arms control. There are many times when it is important to stand firm. Congressional support for a firm stand on any given issue is something the Soviets seldom fail to take into account. Indeed, it may on occasion be one of the least expensive and more persuasive "bargaining chips" an American delegation can take to the negotiating table.

5. Greater congressional involvement during negotiations increases the chance that fallback positions will be leaked.

This may be true, but the weight of this consideration is much less than it would appear. Some fallback positions on minor issues that are included in a delegation's instructions reflect efforts to placate elements of the bureaucracy, or allies, by making a "college try" for their pet ideas; these are positions a government expects to fall by the wayside. Fallbacks from such positions are less likely to be leaked, but in any event they are seldom moving elements in a negotiation.

Regarding the more important and contentious issues, it is useful to consider the real world as opposed to that of the theorists. Presidents, who traditionally regard the bureaucracy as something of a sieve, have always been reluctant to include important fallback positions in a delegation's written instructions unless they are merely part of a plan to regulate the tempo of the negotiation or are inherent in the logic of the negotiating situation. As for the real fallback positions, those resorted to only after a serious and lengthy attempt to achieve initial positions, a president or secretary of state may have some in mind, but he will seldom commit them to paper until he decides to make his move. Thus, in practice the fallback positions the highest officials share with the bureaucracy, with very few exceptions, do not represent vital elements of a negotiation, and the leaking of them that might result from greater congressional knowledge of a negotiation would not seriously damage U.S. interests.

6. *Without benefit of the numerous technical studies conducted within the executive branch, the public and Congress cannot intelligently assess strategic arms control questions.*

A certain mystique was fostered in the early days of SALT about the voluminous interagency studies conducted in connection with the talks. Obviously, technical studies can be helpful and on occasion are necessary in forming judgments. But it is important not to accept with unskeptical awe the assertion that such studies produced unique wisdom on the part of decision makers, or were even in most cases relevant to their decisions. One can grant the sincerity of an administration's desire to assemble and analyze facts and still note that historically one principal purpose of study exercises has been to keep the bureaucracy occupied.

Policymakers in the executive are no less occupied with other problems besides SALT than congressmen or members of the informed public. If one is to judge from the past, for the most part the only officials who read the lengthy SALT studies were the staff members who wrote them. While the negotiator, with his responsibilities more focused, usually managed to read the "Executive Summaries" of such studies, the National Security Council or Verification Panel member who managed to do the same was an exception.

This, however, is not the only or even the principal reason why senior officials with equal access to technical studies often differ in their recommendations. The various influences that affect decision makers in the executive branch have been discussed in recent literature on this subject, but strikingly prevalent in the postwar history of arms control is the influence of what Alexander George calls "decisional premises."[18] The values and beliefs that decision makers bring with them to the meeting room have been far more important determinants of their views on arms control questions than the expert analyses that administrations are prone to point to, but not reveal, while claiming special if not exclusive wisdom.

Thus, despite the technical aspects of strategic arms control, the major issues in this field, once clarified, involve relatively basic (if sometimes difficult) choices that are essentially political decisions. While Constitutional responsibility for such decisions rests more directly on the president and his advisers, special competence for such political decisions is less a reality than a myth. Access to facts, specific knowledge of the issues involved in a negotiation, and the opportunity to reflect on them—all these are necessary for broader public and congressional participation. Exclusive executive wisdom stemming from voluminous interagency studies, however, is not a valid argument against broader participation in this area of public policy.

This does not mean that considerable improvement in the resources available to Congress is not desirable. Access under appropriate arrangements to the analytical capability of ACDA as well as to the considerations influencing the resolution of issues would be helpful.[19] Greater use of the resources of the Congressional Office of Technology Assessment would also reduce the present inequality of resources available to the two branches in this area. Of perhaps even greater practical importance would be enlargement of congressional committee staff facilities. However, the strengthening of congressional capabilities, possibly including the reorganization and con-solidation of committee responsibilities,[20] is not likely to be effective if there is a return to the secrecy that surrounded past SALT negotiations.

7. *More open negotiations would be advantageous to the Soviets, for they would seek to influence public and congressional opinion and thereby exert pressure on United States positions.*

If there is much substance to this argument, the question naturally arises why has Moscow favored secret negotiations? In fact, when Moscow feels it would be propitious to lift the veil surrounding a major issue, it has not felt precluded from doing

so. The rapid disclosure during SALT I of the Soviet proposal
to reach an agreement first on ABMs is a case in point. There
may be some marginal increase in the Soviet capacity to
influence U.S. policy in this manner. Again, however, this
consideration must be weighed against those favoring greater
openness. Democracy has always involved complications with
which closed societies are not burdened.

On the other hand, it is also possible, perhaps even probable,
that more openness will result in more equal opportunities to
influence public opinion in the two countries and, in doing so,
will improve the prospects for arms control. The immensely
less pluralistic nature of Soviet society and the severely limited
opportunities for forces outside a small corps within the
official hierarchy to influence policy present obvious difficulties. Nevertheless, issues of priority exist there as they do here.
There are Soviet (as well as American) mayors who seek
reallocation of resources, and some of those mayors are
members of the Central Committee. Differences over arms
control policy among Soviet officials have been evident at
SALT. Some American observers have suggested that the
SALT process might modify the existing compartmentaliza-
tion within the Soviet government regarding strategic arms
information and policy. Whatever change may have occurred
so far, it is unlikely to extend much beyond officials directly
involved in the negotiations so long as negotiations are secret. I
do not think it naive to consider the possibility that more open
negotiations might expand the circle of influence within the
Soviet Union. We are not without encouraging historical
evidence. Widespread concern about radioactive fallout in the
Soviet scientific community significantly strengthened the
forces in Moscow seeking a nuclear test ban; while we cannot
document this, it appears that the strength of this sentiment in
the scientific community played a part in Khrushchev's offer of
three annual on-site inspections in the interest of achieving a
comprehensive test ban. A significant redirection of current
trends in armament will require a far greater mobilization of
support for arms control than currently exists, both in this
country and in the Soviet Union. There even more than here,
secret negotiations stand as a barrier to progress.

If, as I believe, the seven foregoing arguments are the principal ones supporting secret negotiations, they do not constitute a convincing case. The arguments supporting a more open process are more substantial.

The most compelling argument for less secrecy is that past secrecy has led to an abridgment of the democratic process in an area affecting national security, general foreign policy, and such domestic issues as the allocation of resources and the cost of government. In this nation we have traditionally placed the processes of democratic government before the substance of particular policy questions. The secret nature of past arms negotiations constituted a reversal of that order of values. To secure a more stable and less costly strategic environment and to bring the strategic arms race under control will require major political decisions, not debates among weapons experts and diplomats. Such broad political questions belong in the public arena, not behind closed doors.

SALT, moreover, extends beyond arms control issues. One of the major questions of foreign policy will continue to be U.S.–Soviet détente. Differences regarding its proper scope and judgments about its success vary from person to person. Zbigniew Brzezinski, who has had reservations about Soviet détente policy, has expressed what is probably a widely held view, that the results of SALT should be regarded as a "major litmus test" of Soviet intentions.[21] How can such a litmus test be properly evaluated if secret negotiations conceal what both sides contribute to a given result? If a result is unsatisfactory, we need to be sure there are not undisclosed factors that would alter the nation's judgment; if judgment requires action of some consequence, we need a broad base of political agreement, which is attainable only through more open negotiation.

To the extent that large expenditures of federal funds are required to sustain arms programs, we will require, over the long run, a citizenry convinced that all alternatives have been fully explored. Reactions to earlier SALT II efforts show widespread suspicion that an all-out effort had not been made. Moreover, beyond the immediate issue of arms policy, excessive secrecy in arms negotiations will surely aggravate estrangement between government and citizen.

More specific than the government process issue is the indispensability of more open negotiations to improving prospects for effective arms control. Secret negotiations have worked against this objective in the past, and success was obtained in SALT only when a wider application of wisdom and political pressure circumvented the confined debate that secrecy engenders. Future efforts to control the arms race will require discussion, decisions, and actions on a broad rather than a narrow front. As Marshall Shulman has observed, "SALT involves three sets of negotiations: one is between the Soviet Union and the United States, and the other two are internal negotiations within each of the two countries."[22] Prospects for success in all three will be enhanced by a more open process.

Given the pace of technological change, only a determined, broadly supported effort to seek specific, major arms control adjustments is likely to have a significant impact on current trends. And as arms races have motivating forces beyond those relating to hardware and strategic doctrine, so must future efforts encompass the broader considerations which are the proper subject of political debate and decision.[23] There is little prospect for broad public support of arms control efforts if secret negotiations cloud the normal political process.

A more open process, a greater sharing of real responsibility between the executive and Congress, will also allow us to react more quickly and flexibly to fast-paced technological developments. Secret negotiations tend to focus efforts on formal arrangements of a more lasting nature, all of which require time. Presidents are reluctant to accept sole responsibility for short-term, less formal mutual undertakings, which might prevent the momentum of on-going programs from outdistancing the treaty negotiations, particularly when they fear being charged with circumventing the advice and consent of the Senate. (The converse is the understandable congressional suspicion of "bargaining chip" and "hedging" authorizations.) With more open negotiations and a greater degree of congressional participation and responsibility, a major practical problem of controlling arms in an age of rapid technological change can be approached with more sensible realism than is now possible. George Bunn, dean of the Wisconsin Law School, has outlined some possiblities in this area, as well as some historical precedents.[24] "Escrow authorizations" might also be considered as one means of resolving the bargaining chip and hedging problems.

Not only will broader participation and a more open approach give us the greater flexibility we need, it will also improve the chances of making wise decisions. Some reasons for this have been discussed earlier. Here I want to focus on specific shortcomings in the way executive decisions have been reached.

The narrow composition of the National Security Council, a product of the outdated National Security Act of 1947, results in a policy group with an understandable but disproportionate focus on the "national security" aspects of any given arms control issue. Often, though of course not always, this means a focus on military hardware. Yet the arms race and arms control issues involve a much broader range of considerations. It has been suggested that the decision-making body be expanded to include other cabinet officers, and this would be an improvement. But the most effective means of ensuring more broadly based "multiple advocacy" policymaking would be to involve appropriate members of Congress in the process.

One feature of the executive decision-making process that has been neglected in much of the current literature—and is probably inherent in the executive structure—is the tendency of the presidential appointees comprising the National Security Council to avoid a hard debate on issues with the president, or with their colleagues in his presence. Too often, misstatements of fact or faulty inferences go unchallenged, or considerations bearing on an issue are briefly mentioned but are not pressed in the presence of the chief executive. Views are presented more forcefully in written memoranda, but this is no substitute for a hard-fought debate between unfettered advocates of conflicting views. When debates are confined within a small group—as is usually the case during secret negotiations—this weakness of executive decision making is compounded. Only by expanding the base of advocacy and examination beyond the confines of the National Security Council are the key issues in a negotiation likely to receive the close scrutiny indispensable to wise decision making.

The case against secret negotiations and a return to past practice is, I believe, not only substantial but compelling. Only an open process can avoid a serious abridgment of the democratic process in a vital area of public interest. Only an open process allows even the possibility of the fundamental rethinking necessary to halt the strategic arms race and also to prevent nuclear proliferation from getting completely beyond control. What is required is imaginative boldness of the order that created the Marshall Plan and the North Atlantic Treaty. As in those cases, arresting the arms race necessitates open presidential leadership and shared participation and responsibility with Congress while policy is being formulated and during negotiations.

Moving away from secret negotiations has already occasioned, and will continue to occasion, problems of adjustment. This is always the case when improper, malfunctioning arrangements are corrected. In this regard, however, I would recall some words of Benjamin V. Cohen, a former negotiator for the United States and a wise and experienced man in both foreign and domestic affairs:

> Generalizations about national interest and realistic diplomacy no more solve concrete problems than do generalizations about law and morals. It may be conceded that politicians lacking vision and insight on the international scene as on the national scene try to conceal their own inadequacies by appeals to popular passions. . . . Wise statesmen know that public opinion is capable of greater understanding than ordinary politicians and even technical experts are inclined to believe. Leadership with ideas and with the ability of explaining and defending them is an essential ingredient of democracy. The people are interested not only in the soundness of our objectives but even more in the effectiveness of the means chosen to move in the direction of their achievement.[25]

Notes

1. Nicholas de B. Katzenbach, "Foreign Policy, Public Opinion

and Secrecy," *Foreign Affairs* 52 (October 1973): 1-19.

2. *Saturday Review/World,* May 4, 1974.

3. Lest there be misunderstanding, I do not advocate leaking by the bureaucracy. It is neither a proper nor an effective response to the problem. The source of most leaks during SALT I was the White House, notwithstanding administration fulminations, particularly during the Nixon years, on this matter. White House leaks represent conscious decisions by those who largely make the rules regarding classification to place certain information in the public domain for tactical reasons. Lesser officials in the bureaucracy may be faced with questions of conscience. It seems to this writer, however, that there is an inherent dishonesty in leaking by officials who have agreed to accept the existing regulations but who *secretly* violate them. The proper solution is to change the system.

4. U.S., Congress, House, Committee on Foreign Affairs, *Arms Control and Disarmament Agency: Hearings before the Subcommittee on National Security Policy and Scientific Developments,* 93rd Cong., 2d sess., 1974, p. 115.

5. Ibid., p. 141.

6. Ibid., p. 104.

7. Elliot Richardson agreed, adding the pertinent point that part of the obligation of openness "is to let it be understood that a tough call is a tough call and that there are genuinely valid competing considerations on the other side of whatever the Executive branch resolution of the issue was." Ibid., p. 105.

8. It is generally not recognized that a ban on MIRVs for ABMs is contained in the ABM Treaty, in Article V and Agreed Interpretation (F).

9. This is not to say that an agreement became inevitable. It required strenuous efforts and uncommon skills on the part of many of those involved, not the least of which were directed at resolving the highly technical problem of radar limitations. There was also, of course, much shifting of positions (some of which were for the purpose of "pacing" the negotiations) on the exact nature of the low ABM levels before the treaty limitations were set. In part, this shifting on the U.S. side was due to another delayed result of the open debate, congressional opposition to any ABM "area defense," which caused the White House to seek an alternative to its original proposal to limit ABMs to national capitals.

10. For the most extensive, see U.S., Congress, House, Committee on Foreign Affairs, *Multiple Warhead Missiles: Hearings before the Subcommittee on National Security Policy and Scientific Develop-*

ments, 91st Cong., 2d sess., 1970.

11. The rationale advanced was that since production was not verifiable, there should be no limitations; but since the United States, having tested, was the only side that would benefit from this arrangement, the Soviets predictably objected to it.

12. One such potential ally, Senator Hubert Humphrey, later tried unsuccessfully to obtain a Senate resolution more specifically focused on the MIRV problem than the Brooke Resolution.

13. A distinction must be made, of course, between projections and firm knowledge of future Soviet programs. The Soviets' secrecy about their programs has been a major contributor to the arms competition.

14. One possible exception emerges from the agreements establishing detailed procedures for implementing the SALT I accords. These agreements apparently involved some detailing of technical military information that the Soviets preferred to keep classified. This is a special case for which an argument can at least be made, but it is not central to the question at issue here.

15. This fact was never really appreciated by some officials in the Nixon administration, who tended to think they were writing the first chapters in the history of arms control. Thus, they tended to equate what they considered a surprising degree of civility and seriousness on the part of the Soviets with the strict secrecy imposed on SALT.

16. In 1963 Soviet acceptance of the U.S. proposal for a Hot Line agreement came in a statement so full of polemics that after it was delivered, half the American delegation failed to realize that the first U.S.–Soviet arms control agreement of the postwar period was at hand.

17. A somewhat different case is the 1972 Jackson Amendment to the congressional resolution approving the Interim Agreement on offensive strategic arms, which requested the president in negotiating a replacement for the Interim Agreement to seek a treaty that would not limit the United States to levels of intercontinental strategic forces inferior to those provided for the USSR. While different sponsors of the resolution interpreted its meaning very differently, it was seen by some as restricting executive flexibility by setting a standard isolated from any other provisions that might be included in a future agreement. They had a point. In part, however, the amendment's support was a reaction to a lapse of sensitivity on the part of the Nixon administration, which wrote into what was essentially a freeze on missile launcher totals unequal SLBM (Submarine-Launched Ballistic Missile) launcher and submarine numbers "permitted" the two sides. Focused too narrowly on strategic considerations, the Nixon administration showed less sensitivity than Congress to the

fact that SALT was political as well as strategic in nature, and that with both sides possessing nuclear abundance, appearance was almost as important as substance. This case illustrates in yet another way the need to broaden the base of policy input beyond those who tend to think primarily in terms of the hardware aspects of strategic policy.

18. In his close analysis of foreign policymaking, George notes that "ideological values and various cognitive beliefs of policy-makers (what we have called 'decisional premises') may sometimes be so firmly and uniformly held as to surely constrain the choice of policy. . . . Often, however, there are competing values and a variety of decisional premises within the decision-making group." George, "The Case for Multiple Advocacy in Making Foreign Policy," *American Political Science Review* 3 (September 1972): 784.

19. For comments by Bundy and Richardson on this, see *Arms Control and Disarmament Agency: Hearings,* pp. 104-6

20. For Rusk's and Smith's comments on this topic, see ibid., pp. 114, 121-24.

21. "What Kind of Détente?" *Washington Post,* August 4, 1974.

22. Marshall D. Shulman, "SALT: Through the Looking Glass," *Arms Control Today,* February 1974, p. 1.

23. The focus on a narrow set of strategic policy and military hardware questions, the product of both conservative and liberal analyses for the past decade, is one reason for the misguided tendency to leave arms and arms control policy to the experts. Among others, Colin Gray, while admittedly giving unintended "aid and comfort" to conservative arguments on defense policy, points out the variety of motivations and considerations that have been neglected in much recent discussion of the arms race and which underscore the point that issues are broadly political and involve domestic as well as international politics. Gray, "The Urge to Compete: Rationales for Arms Racing," *World Politics* 2 (January 1974): 207-33.

24. George Bunn, "Missile Limitation: By Treaty or Otherwise?" *Columbia Law Review* 70 (January 1970): 1-47.

25. Benjamin V. Cohen, "The Quest for Peace," speech at Dropsie College, Philadelphia, March 17, 1952.

9
A European Perspective

Kurt J. Lauk

The Problem

For most of the last three decades the United States Congress did not assume, in European eyes, an independent, affirmative role in foreign policy decision making. More recently, however, Congress has gained considerable influence in foreign, defense, and arms control policy. This active involvement of the legislative branch of the United States government in these areas is a new phenomenon for European observers, and its Constitutional basis is not easily understood.

As a rule, Europeans have never accorded their legislative branches a central or coequal role in the formulation of foreign or defense policy. Except in periods of political instability, the government's foreign and defense policies have usually been supported by a majority in parliament—usually the same majority which made it possible for that government to hold power in the first place. The need of a democratic European government for a majority's support in parliament makes parliamentary disapproval of the government's foreign and defense policies a very unlikely event; it would amount, in effect, to a vote of no-confidence. Therefore, it is nearly

The author wishes to thank Jack L. Kangas, Lawrence Weiler, and Alan Platt for their comments on an earlier draft of this article.

impossible for the legislative branch to assume an independent policymaking role, and it was not difficult for Western Europe to live comfortably with a United States Congress that appeared to assume little responsibility for arms control and foreign policy. In these areas Congress was seen as a body that essentially rubber-stamped administration policy. This was regarded as almost inherent in the Constitutional system. For more than two decades this relationship between the executive and legislative branches of government has, in European eyes, provided American policy with exemplary reliability, continuity, and consistency. Europeans have been accustomed to assuming that, with respect to foreign and arms control policies, the word of the American president is authoritative. Although there were relatively minor changes and shifts in policy with every change of administration, there was also a basic continuity, which was identified in Europe with the executive's apparent monopoly in foreign and military affairs.

The new congressional role in foreign and arms control policy poses several difficulties for America's allies. It will take some time to adjust to the new situation. Yet it seems certain that Europeans will be much better off if they acknowledge Congress's increased role in policymaking, rather than hoping the legislative branch will just subside or go away. However, it is also important for the United States not to treat increased congressional influence in foreign policymaking simply as a domestic affair. It does have significant consequences for the European allies. The Atlantic Alliance in particular is likely to suffer unless both sides work together and make the adjustments necessary to accommodate the new congressional role. With respect to arms control, the necessary adjustments are complicated by the bilateral arms control negotiations between the United States and the Soviet Union.

From Multilateral to Bilateral Arms Control

During the 1950s most efforts to negotiate arms control measures were between the two military alliances, the North Atlantic Treaty Organization (NATO) and the Warsaw Pact organization.[1] On the NATO side, the United States was the leading actor, but all proposals were thoroughly worked out within the alliance. The European partners had a strong voice and influence on arms control efforts. Yet until 1963 no significant arms control agreement was concluded that involved a NATO or Warsaw Pact country.

The Limited Test Ban Treaty of 1963 between the United States and the Soviet Union represented the first in a series of significant arms control agreements, leading in 1972 to SALT I and in 1974 to the Vladivostok Accord. All these arms control agreements were in essence negotiated bilaterally between the United States and the Soviet Union. None of these agreements, except the Non-Proliferation Treaty, directly affected weapons deployment or force levels in Europe. Also, none of these agreements were rejected by Congress. Some agreements, such as the Limited Test Ban Treaty and to a greater degree SALT I, were criticized in Congress. SALT I, particularly the Interim Agreement on Offensive Weapons, caused critics led by Senator Henry Jackson to propose an amendment that entailed guidelines for SALT II.[2] In the discussion of this amendment, continued security for the American allies in Europe and the maintenance of an extended deterrence there were a major consideration. The Jackson Amendment was passed by Congress and subsequently lent congressional sentiments greater weight during SALT II. However, SALT I itself was neither amended nor rejected by Congress. Thus, as soon as an American president or another representative of the United States had negotiated an agreement or treaty, the consent or ratification of the U.S. Congress seemed in European eyes to be merely a matter of time. None of the domestic debates on arms control or on the ratification of arms control agreements in the United States received widespread attention in Europe. Arms control agreements were discussed by the European allies as they were presented by the executive branch of the United States government. If a NATO ally wanted to voice concern or even to urge a change in a particular provision of an arms control agreement—as was the case during the negotiations for the Non-Proliferation Treaty[3]—its concerns were addressed, and properly so, to the administration. The executive branch was perceived to have sole authority, and to be the source of the consistency needed to lead the Atlantic Alliance.

Through the years the voice of Congress in foreign and defense policy was perceived as negligible. There was no reason to doubt that the foreign, defense, and arms control policies pursued by the United States were supported by a solid majority in Congress, and hence by a majority of the American people. Until the early 1970s European governments felt justified in focusing almost exclusively on the executive branch in assessing or trying to influence the position of the United States. As a rule, Europeans did not know Congress and thought of it, at best, as a labyrinth of committees. They did not think of it as a potentially strong and assertive factor in foreign affairs or arms control. Of course, there was the Mansfield Amendment, calling for a substantial reduction in American troops abroad, including those stationed in Europe.[4] It was brought up for a vote many times in the late 1960s and early 1970s. Its failure merely reconfirmed in European eyes the dominance of the executive branch, although the Mansfield Amendment did help win NATO's assent to beginning negotiations on Mutual Balanced Force Reductions (MBFR) in Central Europe. Generally, the European perception seemed to be confirmed: the foreign policy of the president might be attacked in Congress, but it was never defeated.

Nevertheless, the progress in bilateral arms control agreements between the Soviet Union and the United States has left the European allies in a quandary with respect to American arms control policy. So long as arms control negotiations were multilateral—and the MBFR negotiations still are—the West European nations were participants, but owing mainly to the tremendous complexities of the issues involved, there was little progress and no agreement. Once arms control negotiations focused on specifically defined strategic issues between the two superpowers, more significant arms control agreements have been concluded, but the European allies have had little influence on the outcome even when it had had important consequences for the strategic balance in Europe. The allies have therefore started to pay more attention to the policy-making process in the United States; they want to influence American arms control policy while it is being made. Dealing with the executive branch was complex enough; the recent assertiveness of

Congress has complicated the Europeans' attempt to follow and influence American policy. Moreover, although they want to influence American foreign and arms control policy, they do not want to be accused of interfering unduly with the internal affairs of the United States.

Past Perceptions

Three episodes of the 1960s—the Multilateral Force debate, the Non-Proliferation Treaty negotiations, and the debate on the Antiballistic Missile system (ABM)—will help clarify the then prevailing attitude of most Western European governments toward the involvement of the United States Congress in arms control and foreign policy. This is not to suggest that there has not been a change in the meantime. However, the perceptions of the 1960s and early 1970s can to a large extent still be considered the basis from which more recent congressional initiatives in arms control policy are judged in Western Europe.

The Kennedy administration revived, particularly after the Nassau Agreement with Great Britain in December 1962,[5] the Multilateral Force plan, originally developed late in the Eisenhower administration. The plan was brought up again at a time when most Western European NATO countries were disturbed over recent developments in American nuclear strategy, which were perceived as making the American commitment to European defense questionable. The United States, on the other hand, was trying to use the Multilateral Force (MLF) to prevent nuclear proliferation in Western Europe, specifically the Federal Republic of Germany. The force would consist of a multinationally manned fleet of surface ships carrying Intermediate-Range Ballistic Missiles (IRBMs), commanded by an integrated multinational command and control structure. The release of nuclear warheads in a war situation, however, was to remain, at least for the near future, entirely in the hands of the American president. Many high-ranking people in the Department of State led the Europeans to believe, however, that American control over nuclear warheads need not be permanent, and that the MLF could in effect be regarded as a forerunner for an integrated Western European nuclear force.

The long and often confusing debate about the MLF within the Atlantic Alliance need not be described here. It is, however, most interesting to note that in the European debate the potential importance of Congress for the approval of the MLF plan was almost never an issue. It was not recognized, even by many European political leaders, that for the MLF to become a reality, congressional approval was necessary—and that at no point were the necessary votes in Congress there. The debates waged in European administrations and European parliaments were quite often heated; they focused, however, almost exclusively on the statements and explanations emanating from the executive branch of the United States government. It was simply assumed that Congress would consent to whatever the European and American governments agreed upon. This gross European misjudgment was to a great extent obscured by the demise of the MLF plan long before it ever had to be voted on in Congress, although the Johnson administration's decision to let the MLF die was influenced by its realization that Congress would not support the plan. Since the MLF proposal died without ever going before Congress, Western European countries were not forced to realize that Congress, as a coequal branch of the United States government, was willing and able to exert its influence on questions of nuclear policy and nuclear arrangements, particularly if nuclear proliferation was involved.

The Congress's determination in this area was—and sometimes still is—not seen or understood by many politicians in Western Europe. In the case of the MLF this was particularly true of the German government and to a lesser extent the Italian; the French and British governments opposed the MLF for their own reasons. Thus, the Europeans had never had to face the challenge of trying to get a controversial proposal through a hostile Congress. This lack of experience has resulted in a lack of knowledge of Congress, an ignorance of its philosophy and of how it works.

Given these European perceptions, the U.S. policy change from MLF to the Non-Proliferation Treaty was seen by most

European governments—with the exception of Britain—as a fundamental shift, since they viewed this shift as a change in direction and not as a continuation of the same policy by different means. It was overlooked that Congress had opposed the MLF almost as strongly as it supported nonproliferation. The MLF had seemed attractive to many Europeans because it appeared to give them increased participation in the nuclear decisions. Nonproliferation, by contrast, was viewed as a policy of decreased or null participation, and was therefore seen as a significant shift in United States policy. The American government viewed both the MLF and the Non-Proliferation Treaty as means of retaining control of nuclear policy within the alliance. France rejected the notion of United States–controlled nuclear policy as long as it seemed in any way directed against France's own nuclear independence. Great Britain supported the nonproliferation policy from the beginning; since it already was a nuclear power, it had nothing to lose. Italy and in particular West Germany were very disturbed by this development in U.S. policy. As the history of the Non-Proliferation Treaty negotiations shows, West Germany and Italy, along with a number of other countries in a similar position, signed and ratified the treaty only after the text explicitly provided for the development and use of peaceful nuclear technology and the European Atomic Energy Commission verification issue was satisfactorily settled.

There was no common European perspective on the Non-Proliferation Treaty. The treaty affected different countries differently, and their reactions were accordingly diverse. Nevertheless, the impression was created in many European countries that the United States, partly owing to pressure from Congress, was willing to accept the possibility—as William C. Foster put it—of an "erosion of alliances resulting from the high degree of U.S.–Soviet cooperation which will be required if a nonproliferation program is to be successful."[6]

The strength of congressional support for nonproliferation was generally not realized in Europe. Unless there are distinct differences between the administration and Congress, the influence of Congress on specific foreign policy issues is usually not assessed. Most European analyses of American arms control policy consider only the administration's position, and make no effort to assess congressional sentiments. The way Congress works is too alien to European models, and its influence is very selective and sometimes erratic. Since in European eyes Congress could not be counted on as a constant and predictable influence on United States policy, it was, for all practical purposes, discounted altogether.

Subsequently, those European governments which placed a high political value on not foreclosing the "European Option"[7] were rather disappointed by the vague and over-restrictive language Congress accepted during the ratification hearings on the Non-Proliferation Treaty. Secretary of State Dean Rusk declared: the treaty "does not deal with the problem of European unity, and would not bar succession by a new federated European State to the nuclear status of one of its former components. A new federated European state would have to control all of its external security functions including defense and all foreign policy matters relating to external security, but would not have to be so centralized as to assume all governmental functions."[8]

Several European governments, particularly the German, were disappointed by that statement on the so-called European Option. (The term European Option refers to the possibility of a true "European nuclear force," which could be foreclosed, as some Europeans feared, by the Non-Proliferation Treaty.) Of course, there are many good reasons to doubt that a European nuclear force would fail solely because of the Non-Proliferation Treaty. In any event, there will be no realistic European Option in the foreseeable future. In this context, however, it is important to recognize that the Congress's own firm convictions on this issue were recognized in Europe only after they resulted in the unexpected dashing of some Europeans' hopes. Several European governments were surprised by Congress's taking an independent stand on such an issue irrespective of what the administration was perceived to have promised its Western European allies. The Europeans' surprise was almost entirely due to their ignorance of Congress, but the episode confirmed the European view that Congress was an unpredictable voice on arms control questions.

The debate over ABM has been widely described as a turning point for congressional participation in defense and arms control policy, and a good case can be made that the debate signalled the beginning of an era of congressional assertiveness in foreign policy. The significance of this debate and its ramifications has not been recognized in Europe.

To be sure, there were detailed reports on the debate in the European press. Yet it was predominantly seen as another domestic squabble over a tremendous amount of money between "hawks" and "doves," a familiar pattern most Europeans could easily relate to, one that had been highlighted in Europe largely as a consequence of United States involvement in Vietnam. The debate was not seen as a dramatic indication that Congress was now willing and able to assert a more powerful influence on the shaping of U.S. arms policy. Nor was the educational effect of the debate on many members of Congress generally recognized in Europe. No inferences were drawn for the nuclear strategy of the Atlantic Alliance from the prospective deployment of an ABM system. The implications of the ABM debate for the strategic balance between NATO and Warsaw Pact countries were not discussed in any detail. Nor was it recognized that the intense involvement of Congress in this strategic debate seemed to open a new chapter in the formulation of United States nuclear and arms control policy.

If the ABM debate was a great educational experience for Congress, with a legacy of a new sophistication and knowledge about arms control issues, the very same debate was the point at which most Western European NATO governments lost touch with the complexities and political import of modern arms policy. The United States can be seen as having taken, through the ABM debate, a significant step forward in its capacity to cope with the complexities of nuclear strategy. Except for a few experts, however, the Western European NATO countries did not make an equivalent advance. One of the indirect consequences of Europe's inadequate understanding of the development of American strategic policy seems to have been that during SALT I, the Western European NATO countries were predominantly concerned with the Forward-Based System issue. Other aspects of the strategic balance potentially affected by SALT that were or could be of great importance for Western European security—such as nontransfer and non-circumvention clauses incorporated into SALT agreements, Soviet deployments of new strategic systems not covered by SALT definitions (e. g., the SS-20)—tended to be ignored.[9]

Only recently have the European NATO countries begun to realize the implications of the continuing SALT negotiation for their own security, defense strategy, and arms control policy. Their ability to meet this challenge in part depends on their ability to understand the role of Congress in the making of United States arms control policy. Ironically, though the ABM debate failed to educate Europeans in the realities of modern military strategy, the close vote in Congress confirmed the European view that such matters are best left to the executive branch. This view prevails despite the obvious influence and expertise that such men as Senators Henry Jackson, John Stennis, and Sam Nunn bring to defense and policy issues.

Reassessing the Congressional Role

The growing concentration of foreign policy decision making in the executive branch in general, and in President Nixon's National Security Council in particular, received little attention from Western Europeans, who continued to see this as the normal, reasonable way to conduct foreign affairs. It has not escaped their notice, however, that in the last five years Congress has regained significant influence on foreign policy. As a congressional report evaluating the year 1974 states: "During 1974 Congress continued to reassert its role in the conduct of foreign policy."[10]

The prospect of direct congressional participation in the making of foreign policy leaves many Europeans uneasy. It is not just the ability of Congress to deal effectively with foreign policy that worries them, but above all its ability to provide the needed sense of predictability. The very fact that Henry Kissinger deemed it necessary as secretary of state to point out that the legislative branch is not suited for "the detailed supervision of the day-to-day conduct of diplomacy"[11] made

European governments wonder who could speak with authority about the long-term foreign policy commitments of the United States? And once a foreign policy had been enunciated, how long would it be supported by both branches of government?

At the same time, Congress's regained influence in shaping American foreign policy gave many legislators, as Senator Charles Mathias put it, "a feeling of institutional success and a feeling that Congress is meeting its constitutional obligations."[12] Another member of Congress, however, wisely cautioned, "Congress is designed to be slow and inefficient because it represents the total diversity in this country."[13] This suggests that over time a new balance of power between the executive and legislative branches must be found with respect to formulating foreign and defense policy. From the allies' perspective it is essential that Congress and the president work closely in determining the nature and extent of United States foreign commitments.

From a European perspective there are four particular political dangers connected with the recent assertion of congressional influence on defense policy:

1. It is widely believed in Europe that American foreign policy cannot be conducted successfully if Congress passes laws rigidly restricting the president's capacity to act and react in the international arena.[14] If a crisis arises in Europe, European governments would like the president to be able to take quick, affirmative action. Europe would not like to see the American response dependent on the time-consuming, unpredictable decision-making process in Congress.

2. Congressman Aspin has pointed out that Congress is "most comfortable dealing with national security matters in procedural terms."[15] Most Western European governments would be greatly concerned if Congress invoked technical procedures to modify in any way current commitments to Europe. Generally speaking, the European allies prefer clear-cut decisions on the nature and extent of the American commitment. The problematic interpretation of procedural moves threatens additional insecurity.

3. European governments particularly dislike being con-

fronted with a surprise decision in the area of foreign policy, as happened in early 1974 when Congress abruptly cut off military aid to Turkey. Irrespective of their views on aid to Turkey, most European countries were startled by the influence of the Greek-American grass-roots lobby in the United States. Nor is the great influence of other lobbies, most of which are unknown in Europe, on congressional decisions really understood in Europe, where there exist no comparable organizations. The potential power of lobbies lends further conviction to the European view that Congress is an unpredictable partner in foreign affairs.

4. Finally, European governments would have great difficulty assessing the direction of American foreign policy if Congress frequently countermands presidential decisions. Although the European allies may sometimes prefer the congressional decision—Congress's refusal in June 1977 to support the president's decision to pull out American ground forces in South Korea is a case in point[16]—it nevertheless is awkward for an ally of the United States to contend with two independent centers of foreign policy decision making in the United States. It tends to devalue a presidential foreign policy decision and undercut its effectiveness. At the same time, this disadavantage is not offset by a clear congressional concept of foreign policy. To Europeans, Congress often seems to be acting quite erratically and without much concern for consistency when asserting itself in foreign policy and defense issues.

One should not conclude, however, that European interests are opposed in principle to a strong congressional role in these areas. Europe merely has a strong preference for the kind of continuity that has in the past resulted from the executive's dominance of policymaking. As long as congressional involvement in foreign and defense policy cannot provide such continuity, it can be argued that having two independent sources of foreign policy decisions is inconsistent with the United States's leadership role in the Atlantic Alliance. The European allies want to see a single U.S. policy that is solidly supported by a majority of the American people. Overall, during the period of executive dominance of foreign and defense policymaking, European interests have been preserved and Europe has prospered. For all practical purposes, therefore, Europe probably would have preferred to see the rarely challenged presidential leadership in these areas continue. Allied European governments are comfortable dealing with the American executive, whereas Congress is essentially an unknown entity. Congress is also a very complex, heterogeneous body, and its current moods and policy stands are extremely difficult for Europeans to assess. Yet it is now understood in Europe that the traditional authority of the president in foreign and defense policy is no longer unchallenged by either Congress or the American people. European governments are now learning to deal with the new situation. They already have accepted the fact that congressional influence is a factor they must reckon with in assessing United States policy. At the same time, given congressional votes on several proposals of the Carter administration—notably the proposed withdrawal of troops from South Korea—the participation of Congress in policymaking is starting to be viewed more favorably in Europe. Yet in the future, the degree of predictability in American policy that Europeans feel they must have can only be maintained if Congress and the executive work more closely together.

Prospects for the Future

Europeans now believe that the arms control negotiations between the United States and the Soviet Union, as well as within Europe, are becoming increasingly difficult, and we question whether they can be continued successfully. The role of Congress in arms control heightens European uncertainty. Congress can influence the future of arms control in two ways. It can insist that the next phase be concluded as expeditiously as possible, even if it means making major concessions that would, in the case of the Backfire bomber and cruise missiles, be more disadvantageous to Europe than to the United States. Or Congress can make the conclusion of SALT II more difficult, by insisting on absolute verifiability and demanding that the effects of the next SALT agreement on the European nuclear theater be carefully considered. It can demand further that no arms control agreement be signed that is perceived by the

European NATO countries as affecting their interests unfavorably.

Given this context of uncertainty about which way Congress will go with respect to arms control, Europeans also ask whether the current assertiveness of Congress is permanent or transitory. The current disposition in Europe is to "wait and see." The current round of SALT has thus taken on special significance in European eyes. Arms control appears to have a high priority within the Carter administration. The anticipated congressional debate on any agreements the Americans conclude will become a test of the strength and direction of congressional influence on American foreign policy. And if it should prove that Congress will be assuming a more direct role in arms control policy—possibly even rejecting a SALT agreement signed by the administration—then the European allies will have to assess again the impact of congressional involvement on the predictability of American policy.

The recent record of congressional actions in the field of foreign and arms control policy is not conclusive. It is not yet clear, for instance, to what extent Congress will consider European interests if it should mean significantly greater difficulties in the bilateral relationship with the Soviet Union. Some recent legislative initiatives should be recalled: Congress made trade expansion with the Soviet Union dependent on a more liberal Soviet emigration policy; the Turkish invasion of Cyprus led Congress to cut off military aid to Turkey; Congress voiced concern about aspects of the administration's Middle East policy, particularly the sale of Hawk missiles to Jordan; Congress also placed controls on the sale of highly sophisticated military equipment to high-tension areas like the Persian Gulf; finally, Congress opposed Kissinger's Angola policy and cut off military aid to that African country.[17]

Without discussing the political merits of Congress's action on Angola, the decision had a more or less procedural aspect that seems especially worrisome in European eyes. The question is one of internal congressional politics: how could a young senator (John Tunney) without sigificant experience in foreign affairs, a man who "did not serve on any of the key Senate committees which oversee foreign affairs and defense matters" become "a central figure in the effort to cut off aid to Angola"?[18] What troubles a European observer in this case is that a senator could assume—apparently mainly because his reelection campaign at home was in trouble and he therefore needed nationwide exposure—congressional leadership in a very sensitive foreign policy arena. Europeans must wonder whether for similar reasons or other reasons stemming from congressional procedures, another senator inexperienced in foreign policy could exert a decisive influence on a critical decision concerning, say, the military or economic support of a NATO ally in time of crisis. Possibly the Angola decision reflected congressional reaction to Vietnam rather than Senator Tunney's influence. Even so, he was able to exploit that sentiment. The knowledge that Congress works this way is by no means reassuring to American allies.

Nevertheless, Western European countries will have to learn to distinguish between process and content in congressional decision making. The involvement of Congress in foreign policy and arms control decisions makes the analysis more complex and problematic for Europeans. Not only does thorough knowledge of the executive branch no longer suffice, but the patterns of leadership within Congress itself have recently become much more obscure. Over the last decade or so there has been a marked decline in the almost unchallenged domination of congressional leaders and committee chairmen over their respective realms. Leadership has become a matter of constant, issue-by-issue persuasion and coalition building The party caucus now provides a forum for dissidents and challenges to the leadership. Devolution of authority to subcommittee chairmen has created more independent actors and centers of authority within Congress. European analysts will have to learn much more about how Congress works and how people in Congress function and think. The interplay between the executive and legislative branches in the period before an issue comes to a vote further complicates the picture. In addition to becoming more complex, decision making is probably also becoming more unpredictable. This seems to be true with respect both to the leading actors involved in a specific decision and to the types of issue traded off against each other at a particular moment by procedural means. For example, an arms control issue affecting Western Europe's security might come to a vote within a procedural context that makes it very difficult for an observer to predict the outcome. In other words, as far as many Europeans are concerned, congressional decision making is unpredictable decision making, and hence inconsistent with United States leadership of the Atlantic Alliance. It will be difficult indeed for the alliance if Congress announces an arms control policy that differs from the administration's.

The allies of the United States will have to change their approach to influencing American positions on issues that affect them. In the future it will not suffice to talk to representatives of the executive branch; a foreign country wanting to influence a specific decision will also have to work through Congress. This will impose an additional demand on the time of already hard-pressed legislators—a demand many of them will find difficult to accommodate.

For leaders of European countries it most likely will not suffice to consult the president on vital issues; they will also have to hold discussions with congressional leaders, with chairmen of committees and subcommittees. This can become quite difficult, since they will have first to ascertain who wields decisive influence on a particular issue at a particular time. To some extent members of the alliance must now become experts on Congress, at least to a greater extent than they have been in the past. Furthermore, a more active pursuit of Congress is likely to complicate European relations with the executive, particularly when the two branches of government are controlled by different parties. The president and Congress will have to coordinate their foreign, defense, and arms control policies at least on fundamental questions to avoid having the United States speak with two voices in the international arena. Congress and the executive should have the same overall priorities in these areas, or America's allies will feel terribly confused and ultimately insecure. Speaking with two voices would create the impression of a fundamental inconsistency in U.S. policy and might even lead abroad to the impression of a weak and indecisive United States government.

The actual content of congressional arms decisions is more difficult to assess. However, a number of likely issues can be deciphered. Nuclear proliferation is again looming high among congressional priorities. At the same time quite a number of weapon systems are due for replacement in Western Europe. In order to maintain the credibility of an adequate nuclear deterrent in the European theater, continuation of the "Two-Key" system—i.e., the physical release of tactical nuclear weapons located in Germany requires, after their use has been authorized, a joint action by an American and a German soldier, each holding a key—will become crucial. Congress might use its influence to discontinue the "Two-Key" arrangements in the cause of nonproliferation. This could be seen as in the interest of the United States. Such a decision might also facilitate progress in the bilateral arms control negotiations with the Soviet Union. Furthermore, such a decision might be made in the name of consistency; for example, how could the United States tell South Korea not to go nuclear, while withdrawing American ground forces from Korea and continuing the "Two-Key" system in Europe?

Another aspect has to be borne in mind. It is in Europe's interest to oppose the congressional tendency to link military issues with other issues. For example, Congress might be tempted to adjust the level of American military deployments in Europe in accordance with the level of compliance by European governments on the question of nuclear proliferation. Such a decision by Congress might have disastrous consequences for the cohesion of the alliance.

A last point should be mentioned. Superficially, it might seem that the more hawkish Congress is, the better European interests are served. Given the current policy of relaxation in Europe, this is not necessarily so. Several European NATO members, such as Greece, Italy, Denmark, and the Netherlands, need détente in order to justify their continued membership in the alliance to their citizens. This is particularly true for countries that have a socialist or communist party in the ruling coalition.

In conclusion, however, it should be emphasized that overall, despite the dangers involved in greater congressional influence on foreign policy, Europeans do not have to view this as a wholly negative development. Several points should be borne in mind in order to avoid unnecessary tensions in the Atlantic Alliance. First, the Constitutional roles of the legislative branch in European democracies and in the United States are very different. Europeans have never accorded the legislative branch a similar coequal role in foreign and defense policy. This is neither good nor bad, but it helps explain Europeans' slowness to understand Congress's increasing voice in foreign policy. Second, for a long time the role of Congress in arms control was not understood in Europe. Before the early 1960s Congress did not seem to be an independent factor in American policy. During the 1960s congressional sentiments on several issues—the MLF, Non-Proliferation Treaty, and ABM—became very strong, but were not recognized as such in Europe. Increased congressional influence on American arms control policy after 1969 and its increased importance for Europe were realized only very late. Thus today European countries have very little experience of dealing effectively with Congress as an independent force in American policymaking, and they will have to make a greater effort to get to know Congress. Third, increased congressional influence carries with it increased congressional responsibility. Congress should not act in a way that disrupts the continuity of American policy or impairs the president's ability to react quickly and decisively in an international crisis. Fourth, the new congressional role requires the executive and legislative branches of the United States government to reduce adversary relations to a minimum. This is essential to the continued effectiveness of American policy. The overall priorities of the executive and legislative branches must be identical.

The task of influencing American policy will be complicated for Europeans. With the joint but independent support of both branches of government, however, they will have the assurance they require of dependable American support for their position.

Notes

1. For a history of arms control and disarmament negotiations during the 1950s, see Bernhard G. Bechoefer, *Postwar Negotiations for Arms Control* (Washington, D.C., 1961).

2. For the text of the Jackson Amendment, see *Congressional Record*, September 14, 1972, S-14870 (daily ed.).

3. For a brief summary of the NPT negotiations, see John H. Barton and Lawrence D. Weiler, eds. *International Arms Control, Issues and Agreements* (Stanford, Calif., 1976), pp. 295-301.

4. Cf. U.S., Congress, Senate, Committee on Foreign Relations, *Hearings: U.S. Forces in Europe,* 93rd Cong., 1st sess., 1973, especially pp. 3-4.

5. Cf. Stanley Hoffmann, *Gulliver's Troubles or the Setting of American Foreign Policy* (New York, 1968) pp. 166, 395.

6. William C. Foster, "New Directions in Arms Control and Disarmament," *Foreign Affairs* 43 (July 1965): 600.

7. For a more detailed discussion of the NPT and its effect on the "European Option," see Kurt J. Lauk, *Die Nuklearen Optionen der Bundesrepublik Deutschland, Die Sicherheit der Bundesrepublik im Kräftefeld der Nuklearen Strategien der Westlischen Nuklearmächte* (Ph. D. diss., University of Kiel, West Germany), pp. 86-89 (publication forthcoming).

8. U.S., Arms Control and Disarmament Agency, Report by Secretary of State Rusk to President Johnson on the Non-Proliferation Treaty, July 2, 1968, in *Documents on Disarmament 1968* (Washington, D.C., 1969), p. 477.

9. For a detailed discussion of SALT and its effect on the Euro-strategic balance, see Richard Burt, "Technology and East-West Arms Control," *International Affairs* (London) 53 (January 1977): 51-72.

10. U.S., Congress, House, Committee on International Relations, *Congress and Foreign Policy: 1974* (Report prepared by the Foreign Affairs Division, Congressional Research Service), 94th Cong., 1st sess., 1975, p. 1.

11. Secretary of State Henry Kissinger, "A New National Partnership," address before the Los Angeles World Affairs Council, January 24, 1975, in *Department of State Bulletin*, February 17, 1975, p. 203.

12. Quoted in *Time* (European edition), June 9, 1975, p. 37.

13. Ibid.

14. The efforts of some members of Congress to limit the president's ability to decide on a nuclear first-strike without the consent of leading members of Congress is an example.

15. Les Aspin, "The Defense Budget and Foreign Policy: The Role of Congress," *Daedalus* 104 (Summer 1975): 167.

16. Cf. Graham Hovey, "Senate Bars Support For a Korea Pullout," *New York Times,* June 17, 1977.

17. See also Neil C. Livingstone and Manfred von Nordheim, "The United States Congress and the Angola Crisis," *Strategic Review* 5 (Spring 1977): 34-35.

18. Ibid., p. 38.

10
How Congress Can Shape Arms Control

Alan Cranston

To talk about arms control is to talk about national security—indeed, survival. Arms control is not confined to strategic arms limitation. It embraces a whole range of national security issues, such as the international transfer of conventional arms, environmental warfare, the spread of nuclear power reactors, and the potential access to nuclear weapons by additional nations and groups within nations.

Congress, an institution with at times fuzzy jurisdictional boundaries among a welter of committees, looks at arms control from several different vantage points. There are three broad areas in which Congress can influence arms control policy: the policymaking process itself; negotiations; and approving (or disapproving) arms control agreements negotiated by the executive.

Policymaking and negotiation are, of course, interrelated. A decision in the policymaking stage can affect the pace, direction, or outcome of negotiations. In turn, developments at the negotiating table can influence policy deliberations. Throughout the entire policymaking and negotiation phases, the third area—the ultimate need to gain public and congressional support for an agreement—must always be carefully considered. Policymaking for arms control, by and large, is an executive branch function. Within the executive branch, the Arms Control and Disarmament Agency (ACDA) has as its prime responsibility the formulation of arms control policies and perspectives. But it provides only one element in the process, and not necessarily the most important element. The Defense Department, the intelligence community, the State Department, and the Joint Chiefs of Staff also contribute. Over all of them are the National Security Council and the president.

Formulating strategic arms control policy is dependent on the collection and evaluation of intelligence data, the pace and direction of ongoing negotiations, the size and character of the U.S. strategic nuclear forces, and the status of United States–Soviet relations in general.

Congress must depend on the executive branch for most of the relevant information on at least the first two of these factors. Thus, Congress can have only very limited influence on emerging arms control policy without adequate sharing of information by the executive branch. Congress has the most influence over arms policymaking in the area of weapons procurement. Through its annual defense budget authorization and appropriations processes, Congress can to some extent codify the overall strategy governing the acquisition and deployment of weapons systems. But, at least until now, the idea of integrating arms control considerations into defense policy decisions has not been in any sense a significant factor.

Congress has attempted to legislate that kind of integration. The requirement that arms control impact statements be provided with requests for funds for weapons systems is intended to provide Congress—and policymakers in the executive branch—with information on weapons systems from an arms control perspective. In this way both branches of government can weigh the arms control impact, along with military considerations, in considering requests for funds. The law merely calls for a statement on the general impact of the weapons systems on "arms control policy and negotiation." It does not require specific information on what effect a particular weapons system may have, for example, on SALT or on prospects for control of conventional arms transfers. Nor does it offer detailed guidelines on the information that would be most useful.

To date, the impact statements have been a disappointment.

The Senate Foreign Relations Committee found that the Fiscal Year 1977 statements "do not comply with the law and are unacceptable as a model for future submission."

If such impact statements are to enhance Congress's influence on arms control policy, there will have to be:

1. informal negotiations between appropriate administration and congressional officials to agree on the most useful form and substance of impact statements;
2. changes in the law to require more specific information in impact statements; and
3. the capacity for Congress to prepare its own arms control impact statements.

Each of these steps would strengthen the role of Congress in arms control policymaking.

Congress also has the power to influence arms control by changing the statutory charters of the appropriate executive branch agencies. For example, Congress could enhance arms control by legislating a stronger voice for ACDA within the executive branch. In 1974 it was proposed that ACDA prepare the arms control impact statements on weapons systems; at present the National Security Council prepares these statements. The objection was raised that giving ACDA this role would put it in the position of judging other agencies' programs and lead to an undesirable adversary relationship among executive branch agencies. This argument would probably be made against any effort to strengthen ACDA's role in internal policymaking. Despite these potential problems, I believe ACDA should be strengthened. I don't think the prospect of making our one central arms control agency a "super agency" is an undesirable one.

Congress can express its concern over arms control in other ways. For instance, Congress has continued to revise the Arms Export Control Act to try to make the United States Foreign Military Sales program (FMS) more consistent with our stated goal of limiting the international flow of conventional arms. The revised Arms Export Control Act also provides, through the so-called Nelson Amendment of 1974, that Congress can block the sale of a specific weapons system to a foreign country by passing a concurrent resolution of disapproval within thirty days of receiving notification of the proposed sale. To date, this power has never been exercised.

On the other hand, congressional threats to apply the Nelson Amendment have contributed to executive reevaluation of some proposed sales, such as the 1976 sale of Hawk missiles to Jordan and the 1977 sale of E3A Airborne Warning and Control System (AWACS) aircraft to Iran. This method is limited in major ways, however. Weapons sales below the $25 million level are not subject to the Nelson Amendment. Further, a crowded congressional calendar and the complexity of any major weapons sale work against passage of a concurrent resolution of disapproval within the thirty days provided by the law.

Congress has also attempted to influence the complex field of nuclear exports, which means balancing such factors as the world energy supply, the nuclear industry's commercial needs, trade relations, arms control, and security relationships. The worldwide energy shortage has accelerated reliance on nuclear power, which increases the danger that either terrorist groups or individual countries might acquire nuclear weapons by clandestine diversion or outright seizure of nuclear materials.

The 94th Congress tied military assistance and FMS credits to certain standards of behavior in the nuclear field. In accord with the Symington Amendment to the International Security Assistance and Arms Export Control Act of 1976, the United States will not provide military assistance or FMS credits to a country that has acquired a nuclear facility but does not take precautions against its being used to make bombs. In August 1976 then Secretary of State Henry Kissinger used this provision to discourage Pakistan from purchasing a nuclear fuel reprocessing plant from France, informing the Pakistani government that the United States might not provide the A-7 aircraft Pakistan wanted if it acquired the reprocessing plant. Neither the French nuclear sale nor the American aircraft sale has even been consummated.

The device of the congressional resolution can also be used to suggest substantive approaches to arms control policy. In

March 1970 the Senate approved the Brooke Resolution, calling for a moratorium on MIRV flight testing. It was reported that a MIRV testing moratorium was actually discussed at SALT I, but the relationship of the Brooke Resolution to such discussions is not clear. A congressional resolution lacks the force of law. An administration is not obliged to follow the mere advice of Congress, and since Congress has only limited access to the content of secret negotiations, a resolution may be incompatible with evolving U.S. policy.

From all this, one can draw a number of conclusions. A congressional role in policymaking is hampered by limited access to vital information. Without its own intelligence sources or access to arms negotiations themselves, Congress must operate in something of a vacuum. This accounts for the ineffectiveness of many congressional policymaking attempts. I do think the concern some people have expressed about the ability of Congress to deal with highly secret information is overblown. Legitimate secret information must and can be kept secret, but there should be an absolute minimum of secrecy in a democracy, and the public should participate in the consideration of matters affecting their security and survival.

Another problem affecting Congress's role—integration of an arms control perspective into all relevant policy deliberations—will remain difficult as long as congressional responsibility is fragmented among too many committees. The trend in reform of the legislative branch is to streamline the committee system, and it has been suggested that a joint congressional committee on national security be formed as a counterpart to the National Security Council in the executive branch. It has also been suggested that a broader group, focused on "interdependence" between defense and foreign policies, be formed to draw together a wider variety of congressional points of view in order to produce the maximum impact on national security policy. Such major structural changes could conceivably equip Congress to perform a more effective role in policymaking.

The executive branch plays an even more dominant role in the negotiating process than in policymaking, in terms of both initiating and conducting negotiations. Until recently, Congress had no direct role in the SALT negotiations. In 1977, however, members of Congress were appointed for the first time as advisers to SALT II and many have since attended negotiating sessions in Geneva. This does increase Congress's knowledge and involvement in negotiations, but it does not give Congress a consistent voice at the negotiating table. Increased congressional participation in negotiations has both practical and institutional limits. It would be both impractical and, presumably, unconstitutional, for the full Congress to reach an independent negotiating position and dispatch a representative to the negotiating sessions to bargain for that position. Continued, even if intermittent, participation by members of Congress in negotiations, coupled with the traditional procedure of executive branch briefings to the House and Senate Armed Services Committees, and the House International Relations and Senate Foreign Relations Committees on the negotiations, will serve to improve Congress's access to information about this important part of the arms control process.

Congress, through its own procedures, can still influence the negotiating process. One example is passage of congressional resolutions. In 1966 the Pastore Resolution passed the Senate during negotiations on the Non-Proliferation Treaty, and the Humphrey-Dodd Resolution passed the Senate during the 1963 negotiation of the Limited Test Ban Treaty. Both resolutions supported the efforts of the executive branch and served to signal the kind of reception the treaties would receive in Congress. What specific influence these resolutions might have had at the bargaining table is uncertain, of course. In 1977 Senator Edward Kennedy and I reintroduced a resolution calling for a moratorium on all United States underground testing of nuclear weapons and calling on the Soviet Union to follow suit. Our purpose in sponsoring this resolution is to strengthen the president's efforts to gain a formal treaty banning all nuclear testing—at least by the United States and the Soviet Union.

Another congressional tool for influencing negotiations is the confirmation process. To the extent that any chief arms control negotiator affects the course of negotiations, the Senate's approval or disapproval of a specific negotiator can indirectly influence the negotiations.

That both the Senate Foreign Relations Committee and the Senate Armed Services Committee held hearings on Paul Warnke's nomination for this post demonstrated a degree of concern over the choice of a negotiator that had not surfaced before, at least with regard to SALT. Further, the differing perspectives on arms control were reflected in the two committees, with their different jurisdictions. In the debate over Mr. Warnke, Congress, and the Senate in particular, showed how it could shape the parameters of arms control negotiations, even though it has no delegate on the negotiating team. The debate was in many important ways a debate about both the present strategic balance and the contents of any sound arms control agreement. The struggle to confirm Paul Warnke could be considered a dress rehearsal for the struggle over future strategic arms limitation treaties.

In approving Mr. Warnke as chief SALT negotiator by a vote of 58-40, the Senate sent a message regarding the SALT negotiations. If seventy or more senators had voted to confirm Mr. Warnke, this might have signalled Senate receptivity to early approval of almost any SALT treaty, even one perhaps involving unilateral initiatives on the part of the United States. On the other hand, failure to approve this nomination by, say, one vote would have signalled the Senate's hostility toward SALT and the probability that any arms limitation treaty would be rejected.

Perhaps the signal sent by fifty-eight votes for Warnke was just about right. That is, it would seem to indicate that a significant majority of the Senate supports the president in his choice of chief negotiator, has a substantial interest in progress in arms control negotiations, but will critically examine any treaty in terms of its soundness, its equity, and its verification provisions. Thus, in debating the confirmation of a presidential nomination, the Senate indeed was shaping the future of arms control by shaping the perceptions of leaders in both the United States and the Soviet Union.

The Senate has other indirect ways of influencing at least

the climate for arms control through actions in related areas. On March 23, 1977, a substantial majority of senators signed a letter to President Carter endorsing his human rights stand. This action can be seen as a step toward a general foreign policy consensus that would support the president in future major initiatives such as a SALT II treaty. That is to say, when conservative, liberal, and moderate senators alike find much that they can strongly identify with in foreign policy, this contributes to a policy coalition that may make possible significant new initiatives by the president as he strives to reduce the danger of nuclear war.

Another immediate way the Senate can influence the future of arms control is to critically examine the contents of the SALT proposals made by both sides. It is sometimes useful to float a trial balloon in the Senate in order to test sentiment in Congress and the executive branch and in the country. I tried to do this in 1977 with my "Vladivostok plus" proposal, which suggested that the United States negotiate a SALT II treaty including both the limitations of the Vladivostok Accord and two additional limitations: the United States would agree to interrupt development and testing of sea-launched and ground-launched cruise missiles and agree to range limitations on the Air-Launched Cruise Missile (ALCM). In return, the Soviet Union would be asked to agree to stop development of its mobile ICBMs and curb development of the Backfire bomber so that it could not be used as an intercontinental strategic bomber against the United States.

The final act in U.S. adherence to any arms control agreement is the sole responsibility of the Senate, and it theoretically provides the greatest and most unique opportunity for Congress to play a significant part in arms control. But again, there are limits to what Congress can do. In practical terms, the Senate has the option of either rejecting or accepting a proposed treaty. Of course, the Senate can adopt reservations or amendments to treaties, but the former does not bind the other signatories and the latter requires renegotiation of the treaty to gain the signatories' approval. A prudent administration, however, will have taken into account what the Senate is or is not likely to accept. *That* is the greatest opportunity for congressional influence. The Jackson Amendment to the joint congressional resolution approving the Interim Agreement on Offensive Weapons stipulates that United States weapons levels must not be inferior to those of the Soviet Union. At this writing, a SALT II Treaty has not been concluded, and thus the specific effects of this amendment cannot be measured. Congress has many tools with which to influence arms control. None of them is perfect—or particularly effective, experience has shown—when used alone.

But their cumulative effectiveness, when used with skill and proper timing, can be substantial, especially in the hands of the highly skilled craftsmen in Congress. Of course, the will to use these sometimes cumbersome tools must exist and must be strong. Congress can perhaps serve its most effective role as a public forum for new ideas and as a catalyst between the public and its president. Individual members of Congress, if not Congress as a whole, can play a creative, constructive part. And Congress can serve as a collective point-man and help lead, or push, the president toward control and reduction of weapons arsenals—the only alternative to nuclear disaster.

Afterword

John Wilson Lewis

Congress has expanded its role in arms control and international security policymaking under the Carter administration. With power, ideology, and independent judgment displacing party loyalty as governing motives in both the executive and legislative branches, the new Democratic president has made little headway against a Congress controlled by fellow Democrats. Rather, Congress has had a comparatively greater impact on the diverse issues treated in this volume than it had under Presidents Nixon and Ford, and indeed has seemed to become especially forceful with respect to SALT. In 1977, following the Senate's stormy confirmation hearings for Paul Warnke as director of the Arms Control and Disarmament Agency and chief SALT negotiator, the administration tried to neutralize the legislature's pronounced skepticism about negotiations with Moscow and worked to involve Congress more fully than ever. Most dramatic was the effort to inform selected congressional committees of the status of SALT just as negotiations on the Phase Two accords entered a most sensitive stage. Despite the administration's second thoughts on this effort after congressional foes of the treaty used their privileged knowledge as a political weapon, few advocated a return to the old habits of bureaucratic muteness and masquerade. Congress thus seems destined to have an ever greater say in arms control decisions into the 1980s.

This book was conceived at a time when the trends toward

a deeper congressional involvement in arms control matters were well established but the implications of this development were still unclear. The contributors to this volume diverge in their assessment of Congress's more active participation in arms control, but would agree, I believe, that the study of that enhanced role has just begun. It was understood during our discussions of the essays in this book, for example, that the mere possibility of congressional intervention could, in many instances, forestall or alter a president's policy. Few of us foresaw, however, just how early such adjustments by the Carter administration might begin and with what results. Continuing uncertainties about the lasting consequences of such anticipatory moves have suggested a number of new unanswered questions that test our general knowledge of executive-legislative politics. While most of us would probably concur that public policy in this delicate and complex area requires congressional understanding and support, there exists no solid study of workable modalities for this involvement over the long run.

The premature wrangling over an unsettled and delicate negotiation in 1977 did cause a backlash against congressional "meddling" and resurrection of the idea that arms negotiations, in the first instance, are in the preserve of the commander-in-chief. Ironically, calls for restoring the president's primacy in national security matters appeared to originate principally from the Democrats, the more liberal press, and Congress itself. While the criticism spotlighted the early Carter administration's piecemeal and often clumsy foreign policy and its failure to present a persuasive brief for its arms control policies, it also illuminated congressional weaknesses. For congressional intervention often seemed best suited to blocking action, to scoring points, and to using arms control as a means to carve out domains. Those advocating presidential dominance of arms control found their case all the more compelling at a time of widespread apprehension over the weakening military position of the United States vis-à-vis the Soviet Union, over international consequences of advanced generations of conventional and nuclear weapons, and over the potential of a number of pivotal states to enter the nuclear club. Increased ambiguity and complexity of military power in the 1970s—to say nothing of its awesome dangers—seemed to many to require a compensating clarity and coherence in arms control policymaking. The president alone, it was argued, could meet that requirement.

Debate on the proper locus of leadership also sparked a polemic concerning the relative merits of the congressional and executive bureaucracies. Here again the presidency did not automatically come out ahead. Many observers found the members and staffs of several congressional committees better equipped than the executive branch to judge with minimal bias conflicting evaluations of weapons impacts, verification possibilities, and likely military scenarios. In making these crucial assessments, congressional committees frequently proved better prepared and tougher-minded than their administration counterparts. Furthermore, it was Congress, not the executive branch, that pressed to fill the obvious gaps in American knowledge of future security and arms control problems and expressed dismay over the dwindling supply of trained arms control specialists. Many members of Congress, I might add, felt apprehensive about the ramifications of such comparative advantages, if they were real, and acknowledged that in the final analysis, only the president could lead the nation in foreign affairs.

Their apprehension stemmed in part from recognizing the constraints on any legislative body that attempts to execute public policy. Living and working within fluid coalitions, subject to sudden shifts in priorities and unpredictable electoral demands, to say nothing of the fickleness and near chaos of the legislative schedule, Congress cannot be expected by even the most avid arms control advocates on Capitol Hill to play more than a lawmaking role. With so many solons preoccupied with domestic issues and with so few political rewards to be won in the arms control arena, only the most hardy arms controllers might remain fully engaged on a sustained basis. And under these circumstances changes in public mood could become exaggerated on the floor of the Congress and could further complicate sensible arms control policymaking. Inevitably, calls for presidential leadership on arms control and other foreign policy issues are accompanied by complaints about congressional irresponsibility and lack of restraint.

What sometimes has been forgotten during these swings of the judgmental pendulum in the past decade is that Congress is not only permitted but required to act on arms control matters by the Constitution itself. It mandates congressional powers in regard to making war, the military budget, international commerce (including arms sales), and the common defense. The Senate possesses the additional warrant to grant or withhold its advice and consent on relevant appointments and treaties. Legislative "meddling" in arms control is firmly grounded in the Constitution.

The challenge to arms control specialists is to assist the legislature by enhancing its ability to distinguish and diagnose the critical problems. Which problems most urgently require action by Congress, and what issues are central to them? How can questions be formulated to elicit clear and responsive testimony? How can competing technical reports and opinions be made more understandable and more susceptible to knowledgeable evaluation? How can broadly valid judgments about security be sustained in the face of blatant statistics-mongering and superficial expertise? What are the expectable strengths and weaknesses of intelligence estimates, trend analyses, and weapons predictions in general? What are the central *political* issues, issues that fall outside the ken of experts and soothsayers? Finally, how can congressional decisions focus on the major international realities that can and should be debated on Capitol Hill?

In the final analysis, the questions of Congress's proper role in the field of arms control and international security will not be settled by legal formulas or moral pronouncements. James Madison understood this when, in 1788, he wrote to the people of New York on the necessary balance between readiness for war and excessive militarization in peace. "The means of security," he said,

> can only be regulated by the means and dangers of attack. They will, in fact, be ever determined by these rules, and by no others.

It is in vain to oppose constitutional barriers to the impulse of self-preservation. . . . Not the less true is it, that the liberties of Rome proved the final victim of her military triumphs. . . . A standing force, therefore, is a dangerous, at the same time that it may be a necessary, provision.

In the language of today, the weighing of arms build-ups against arms controls requires a persistent, prudent scaling of considerations that can be accomplished, however imperfectly, only with what Madison calls "a due attachment to the Union of America." It was to the Congress, with its many foreseeable inadequacies and its rough-and-tumble approach to decisions, that the Founding Fathers entrusted such an attachment to national unity. For them the search for arms control in an insecure world was connected to the fundamental purpose of remaining free and at peace. They charged Congress with attaining that goal.

Index

F